Stony the Road

Stony the Road

HAROLD J. RECINOS

RESOURCE *Publications* • Eugene, Oregon

STONY THE ROAD

Copyright © 2019 Harold J. Recinos. All rights reserved. Except for brief quotations in critical publications or reviews, no part of this book may be reproduced in any manner without prior written permission from the publisher. Write: Permissions, Wipf and Stock Publishers, 199 W. 8th Ave., Suite 3, Eugene, OR 97401.

Resource Publications
An Imprint of Wipf and Stock Publishers
199 W. 8th Ave., Suite 3
Eugene, OR 97401

www.wipfandstock.com

PAPERBACK ISBN: 978-1-5326-7440-2
HARDCOVER ISBN: 978-1-5326-7441-9
EBOOK ISBN: 978-1-5326-7442-6

Manufactured in the U.S.A.   JANUARY 24, 2019

CONTENTS

The Foreigner | 1
We Shall Overcome | 3
Wake the Dead | 5
Blasphemy | 7
Nieto | 8
Tompkins Square | 9
Steal Away | 11
Dead Friends | 13
Holy Word | 15
White Masks | 16
Wreckage | 18
The Radio | 20
God Bless America | 22
Mountain Top | 24
Heavenly | 25
Enchanted | 26
La Bodega | 28
The Crucified | 30
The Cross | 31
God | 33
Home | 36

The Trump Crusade | 38
The Stone | 40
Migrant Woman | 42
Genesis | 44
Signs | 46
Minutiae | 47
Long Road | 49
Storage | 51
State of the Union | 53
I.C.E. | 55
Morning | 57
My Foster Mother | 59
Grand Child | 61
Come Sunday | 62
The Knock | 64
The Odor | 66
The Scraps | 68
Morning | 70
Another | 72
The Fire Hydrant | 74
The City | 76

Contents

Refugee | 78
Welcome | 80
Shots Fired | 82
Friday | 84
The Stone | 86
Simple | 88
Tell Me | 90
El Norte | 92
The Mission | 94
Good Friday | 96
The Visit | 98
Sunday | 100
The Chalice | 102
The Dream | 103
The Lunch Hour | 105
Impenitent | 107
Carry Us | 109
The Closing | 111
The Take Over | 113
The Knock | 115
Lock Up | 117
Look | 119
Graduation | 121
Animals | 123
Santa Fe Shooting | 125
Another Weeping | 127
The Speaking Tree | 128
The Cure | 130
The Subway Ride | 131

A Clear Day | 133
New World | 135
The Table | 137
The Wreckage | 138
Waiting | 141
The Wait | 143
The Veteran | 145
Simple Matters | 147
Loisaida | 149
Criminalized | 151
Awake | 153
Thorns | 154
Mother Tongue | 156
The Age to Come | 158
Lost Boys | 160
Flowers | 162
Shorty | 163
Jailed | 166
We, the People | 168
The Neighbors | 170
The Party | 172
The Last Days | 174
The Hospital | 176
Taking in the Light | 178
The Border | 180
In My Skin | 182
Kin | 184
Betrayal | 186
Bread | 188

Contents

The Candle | 189
The Line | 191
No Road | 193
The March | 195
Grace | 197
The Toddlers | 199
Heavenly | 201
Hell | 203
The Water | 205
They Cross the Border | 207
Lies | 210
Night | 212
Harmony | 214
Word | 215
Wickedness | 217
Bus Stop | 219
The Island | 220
The Stroll | 221
Cage | 222
Earthly Dust | 224
Posterity | 226
Alphabet City | 228
Rain | 230
Last Breath | 231

Dreamer | 233
Rehab | 235
Faile Street | 237
Esther | 239
Kneel | 241
The Nightmare | 243
Deported | 245
Apartment | 247
Labor Day | 249
The Forgotten | 250
Public School | 252
The Clocks | 254
The Fire | 256
The Judge | 259
Sophia | 261
Heresy | 263
Lord | 265
Sacrilege | 266
The Caravan | 268
The Nationalist | 269
American Pie | 271
Pragmatism | 273
The Sale | 275

THE FOREIGNER

you departed for a city
in another country to a

place you heard of once
beneath the low hanging

branches of a tree. you are
in the caravan of brown faces,

among the mothers with infants,
the youth undoing shackles, the

broken elders hardly able to walk
and the disabled children never

mentioned in American news who
get pushed across the Spanish speaking

borders in old wheelchairs. in the
evening around holes with dancing

flames, the strangers with whom you
walk discuss the hounds barking at the

border, the soldiers in confused wait, the
High-priests so expert at looking the other

way and the English only people who never
imagine the dreams of Christ. we shall

wait in the darkness you left behind hoping
to touch your hand someday, we will pray

in the old village church to the obscure
heaven that one day will make a way for

us, and the candles in front of the blessed
Mother will be kept burning until we are

certain you have crossed the river, safe.
on that day we promise to tell your story

like a sweet biblical tale.

WE SHALL OVERCOME

we shall with courageous faith
stand in the public squares to

face despisers with gargantuan
displays of love. where the wind

blows, we shall march to overcome
the boundaries, the pain, the fear,

the inequalities of these splintering
years. we shall overcome with the

simplicity of tenderness and God's
sublime tears. after all the waiting,

we shall overcome in countless ways
the penetration of nails into our dark

skin, the ignorant mockery of the
Spirit above and the butchery of

Christ's injured love. we shall overcome
the spit in the face, the rubbish they

say and the theologies of hate also
easily preached. we shall overcome

with the colored Christ who came
to give his life for us. soon, and very

soon, we shall overcome with the truth
that hung on a tree.

WAKE THE DEAD

listen to the drums beating
out the sounds of the centuries

beseeching, the tune of snapping
chains, the squealing of tyrants

removed by the nameless, the
revolution that moved into a

White House built by African
slaves, these blood-soaked days

on the impatient earth hosting the
reckless bully with a vacuous brain

who relentlessly throws shit at life.
hear the poor he puts in cages, the

huddled masses to the gale tossed,
the children from across the border

crying about freedom in loathing
disrepair, the black lives stomped

by nationalist cops, confederate
marches full of ignorant white hate,

and America face down in a shameful
shallow grave. what became of liberty,

justice and equality on these American
tongues? What future is prepared now

in the name of Anglo-Saxon superior
myths? what will become of our sons

and daughters when greedy old men
and women are done disemboweling

the people they call filthy illegals and
spics?

BLASPHEMY

I saw you last night in a
tear still talking of things
you love, no less certain
of the world turning ever
so slowly in the direction
of God, recollecting out
loud the humblest times
at a kitchen table sharing
hard bread and talking of old
women in the big church who
pray on its steps with disfigured
hands reaching out to heaven. I
saw you in the tiny drop of water
shared, in your whispered words
telling a truth from someplace
else you say can stop arguments
in the world and you the whole
time promised to take me to this
space even before I renounced
my blasphemy or bothered to
kneel in the dark.

NIETO

on nights like this I bet you
think it's easy to lasso the
stars, drag them behind you
like a kite in the sky and in
deep hours laugh beneath
them until bells ring inside
our limbs. tonight, we will
drink the air with your first
year breath, smile beside you
with clear brows, confess a
world of milk and honey and
feel warm from this June day
for the rest of life. on nights
like this we will sit for hours
with wide-mouthed flowers
sharing perfumed smiles, with
dreams hanging from our eyes,
stories in two languages gushing
from our lips and you Oliver
will know the ancient songs
with certainty flowing in your
saintly blood!

TOMPKINS SQUARE

when the moon rises
above the rooftops I
find time to play with
shadows that make me
think about meeting you
nearly every day on the
same bench in Tompkins
Square park. we talked
of abandoned tenements,
vagabond cats singing into
the early morning dark, new
immigrants squatting in the
empty buildings, the Ukrainians
at tables on first Avenue eating
beet borscht, the hundreds of
hustlers on New York's streets
strumming guitars, entertaining
the public with jokes or begging
to make the next meal. you looked
innocent on the Lower East Side,
a foreigner still dreaming of the

warm sun that pranced the edges
of the rainforest, never troubled
about having no place in the new
world, your voice gently falling
into me and the stars declaring
you alive. I held your clay hand
in mine, loved you completely
and promised to tell the world to
see life in your undocumented
flesh.

STEAL AWAY

I spent many hours walking
the streets, crossing bridges
into other boroughs at night
to get a good look at the city
in glimmering light, feeling
the cool breeze brushing the
dirt from the corduroy jacket
given to me by an elderly Puerto
Rican man who saw me sleeping
alone in the basement behind
Cookies apartment. Often, I
went to the rooftop thinking
about old bible school stories,
imaging it a place like Mount
Sinai, looking for miles in the
dark for a revelation that would
give me endless reasons to hope
and dream. I walked down the
Grand Concourse in shoes with
holes, surrounded by people I
did not know, smiling at the sweet

sound of Spanish dropping from
their tongues, sometimes stopping
on the corner like it was a bank
on the river Jordan where slaves
wept for freedom, to cry like a
captive eager for the Promised
Land. I spent many hours alone
in cities far, near and across a
vast sea, waiting for the sweet
rolling of the river troubled from
above to see me and the earth's
despised children to the other
side.

DEAD FRIENDS

I have survived longer than
the violent nights that left

me with mysterious gifts,
laden with the sound of your

voices that still haunt these
streets and only your sweet

traces know how to penetrate
my darkness. I have spent a

lifetime offering explanations
for the broken worlds God must

see, remembering the names of
our streets, the building numbers,

the public schools, the polished
nails worn by the Puerto Rican

girls, the smell of apartments
with food slowly cooking on

stoves, the Spanish words on cut
paper placed on bedroom altars

full of Saints with otherworldly
looks and the nightmares made

from hellish times. nothing is
like having you roam about in

my dreams, hearing you carefully
tell stories refined in the afterlife

and observing your lewd gestures
for God who took you from these

streets. I still hum the old tunes
we listened to until dawn every

Saturday on the stoop, sit quietly
watching evening shadows sink into

darkness and pray to make the
flowers on the fire escape send

touchable miracles.

HOLY WORD

the preachers of ancient texts
are guiding their thirsty flocks
to the nearest brooks in good
faith. the ungodly campaigns
in the changing hours, rejected
beggars on the church steps,
the forgotten poor with yokes
around their neck, the children
who stumbled away from mud
floor dwellings, mothers at the
gates crying for bread with infants
on their knees, the dry bone voices
filling the air, the innocent who
wait for water to become wine, the
tongues that mock the vulnerable
from sun up till down, hear today
from a preacher's lips a holy word
about infidelities in the world still
delivering God to the cross.

WHITE MASKS

the children in the schoolroom
with old inkwell desks whose eyes

are bigger than curiosity stare at the
neatly pressed white teacher at the front

of the room. they learn to read history
mostly in black and white, while the

deep scars of weaving generations, the
near pulverized first nations, European

land theft, Mexican lynching, yanqui
peasant killing and the politicians who

looked away from black, brown, yellow
and red women raped never appear on a

public book page. the contract historians with
English names, their hard of hearing college

prodigies, never bother to put the bloody
side of colored history in their texts, which

infinitely overflow with grand white stories.
when the children in the class strayed away

from the morning lessons, the teacher
called them back to the lost paradise

text and with not too many words showed
her students how to put on a white mask.

then, one stubborn boy with the habit of
sitting at a desk in the back of the room

yelled, "Teacher, I like it when you call
me, José!"

WRECKAGE

the wind found a little
rest in the pocket of the

old building an inspector
scheduled to condemn just

last week. it has gathered
dust, shouts, sorrows and

joys on the corner over the
years, speaking to the city

in Yiddish, Italian, English
and Spanish always lighting

up the sad dark. we talked
about it standing in front of

Joey's bodega, seeing the
Puerto Rican kids visit the

store tugging at each other's
shirts, sipping from the same

bottle of soda, laughing on
those streets stuffed with family

dreams, and every step taken
by them so completely full

of expectation. Victor once
lived in the condemned building

no one imagined defined by
a clock made from Orchard

Beach sand, the lightest side
of heaven and now about to

be tumbled. we chanted adios
on the way to the alley behind

the tenement, carrying spray
paint cans to write our names

on its wall again in fat twisted
letters.

THE RADIO

in a world with streaks of light
Picasso would have run down

our spines from bulging eyes,
radios announce in crowded

apartments last night's injuries
and remains of those flattened

by devouring white rage. the smug
politicians who find clever ways

to say God, ignore the beggars at
the gates unkind Americans so

carefully raze with their smiling
English only lips and blindness for

the blessed fruit in brown wombs
birthing human beings. in a world that

hates wretched migrants with Spanish
names, in all the places of worship

that never call us fathers, mothers,
brothers, sisters, husbands, wives,

children, neighbors or friends, we
ponder in American English about

soldiers at the border, I.C.E. agents
down the street, cops taking aim, the

work for penny wages, the endless
nights weeping, the disemboweling

of Jesus and American shame!

GOD BLESS AMERICA

the moon is rolled up for
sleep and our dreams are

troubled by the sound of
shouting on the White House

lawn, the rackets on the small
town streets, the corrupt ideas

of pious hearts and the faces
God dares not to see. tonight,

tears wash us clean while the
slow hold of darkness roves

around cursing at the light that
shines in our children's sweet

chocolate faces. tomorrow, we
will awaken within the four walls

of the country's hate, kept from
choice white spaces, trembling

at the image of a cropped-hair
Christ descending from the steeple

of respectable wealthy churches
and wondering how exactly does

God bless this America to which
our kids too sing? Does anyone hear

the varied carols in the nation's
voice, anymore? Does anyone

hear black, brown, yellow and
red faces sing about freedom

and equality too? beloved country
how long will your costly promises

bleed? what will history say about
the disfigured wrong skin bodies

left by white hate to rot with nooses
fixed to their necks? beloved country

I am the murdered, assaulted, raped
and wronged history your very own

God will tell you is blessed!

MOUNTAIN TOP

a memory of a perfect morning
is filled with early Spring scents
that carry you to high mountains
and back, again. the frail flowers
there gently touched by raindrops
from gods in play will draw you
toward the great design where Eden
still gives herself to unmake your
nightmares. the color of our skin and
crisping hair is flawless beauty from
the kindest God. the hands we hold
and magic words pouring from our
fulsome lips sweet elegance to see and
hear. before I die the wind will pull
down the marching white sheets, the
loveless visions and rudderless men
who blow out the candles at heavenly
saint's feet to keep the world dim. I
will not live long enough to cross the
Jordan but when the darkness settles
I will stir from the grave to see it
come.

HEAVENLY

the moon came to the night
in a silvery dress dangling
like a pearl on a necklace in
the heavens. you could hear
the hearts beating on the city
rooftops, the eyelids walked
on the sidewalk slipping into
dreams, the little girls yet on
the stoops taken by the hand
to cross the ancient sky to
shout in the wind. down the
hill by the east river shores the
faint singing of night birds on
the banks could be heard all
night. the raised heads in prayer
understood magnificent times like
this remind us nothing can keep us
from rites of Spring and how they
cough up memories of departed
loves.

ENCHANTED

on Riverside Drive above the
Hudson River a little girl drags

her long skirt along the dusty
sidewalk, an old couple stroll

by looking at the night slowly
climb into heaven and the air

smells like Spring. the benches
along the strip play host to the

city's paupers, pampered dogs
exit the fancy buildings, a few

done up to show, and a kid in
a stroller loosens a huge smile

at the English boxer that licked
his tiny feet. by Grant's tomb

on 122nd Street, a Jazz ensemble
is playing it right, a song people

know better than church, and
that jive about joy coming in the

morning seems true. tonight, the
old city lets us walk up to our waist

in dreams and to these delicious
charms we will return again to

translate inward sorrows into
honied peace.

LA BODEGA

the black dressed old women
in the bodega talk with the grocer

about the days when they feel
like the Holy Mother buying herbs

to make meals for aging boys on
the block, near balding men who

place big food orders for storefront
social clubs, and even a few honest

gumshoe Puerto Rican cops who
spend long nights watching over the

kids on the block. a young man stops
in the corner grocery store to buy

flowers resting in a lonely vase inside
a glass-door refrigerator where tiny

Puerto Rican flags fill a small box
pushed to a corner. Henry's widow

briefly smiles in his direction moved
to know that every Friday Hector

enters the bodega to buy the prettiest
flowers on hand to show his devotion

to a beloved grandmother living in his
apartment who has never bothered to

learn a lick of English. the place is
jumping with people who never consult

academics happy in their far away
homes, theologians offering seminars

about a distant God, and fancy uptown
philosophers uncertain of what to call

black faces, the subtle mysteries of
barrio life, and the spaces where white

words only gasp for air.

THE CRUCIFIED

the nameless people who are
the beautiful brown color of
the earth, those hard at work
for America's gain, who fled
the blade on other shores and
here are daily silenced by hate
will never break. if only you
knew the Spanish they speak
to Angels of a dismayed God,
the freedom that stumbles in
their dreams, the pain in their
limbs, then you would know the
hungering words they speak that
yell darkness in days to come will
sink into the marsh and not a shred
of white wickedness will survive
to hammer into pieces liberty and
justice for them.

THE CROSS

I sat in the small apartment
observing the brown body
on a cross hung on the wall
above a television set begging
the face dripping dark tears
if it's true the trampled who
shout up to heaven will have
life through the Galilean nailed
to a tree. I wondered for hours
about that brown body expiring
on the cross, the crime against a
human being of dark skin displayed
on a hill, a mother who cried for
her dying son, the false charges of
arrest that delivered him with
hands up to suffering and death,
how it all looks like what's daily
going down on inner city streets.
I pondered long the tales of the
Word stooping down into middle
eastern flesh for all who need love,

the calloused men of arrogance and
greed consumed by sin, the ethically
innocent who wait for their dream
world to begin, then prayed for more
than miracles. I sat content to see
Jesus on the blistered wall, holding
in my hand the last look of the mothers
on the block who watched their kids
carried off to jail, those who walked
for hours on the streets and wanted so
badly to meet the loathed brown savior
who like so many black and brown
children meet death on a tree while
elated pale faces dance.

GOD

we looked for god on
Rikers Island getting
stabbed in his sleep,
with ex-dealers in cages
getting GEDS, pocketing
a certificate of completion
for spoken word classes,
or talking on the cellblock
with Tarzan.

we looked for god making
water into wine at the liquor
store, on the moist faces of
dope sniffing kids, in the alley
behind the abandoned
building on Simpson Street
at night taking a good old
wino piss.

we looked for god at the
Ortiz Funeral home where

bitter eyes wept for little
Carmen beaten into silence
by her pimp, in the Gideon
bible Tito lifted at the Days
Inn where his grandmother
cleans all day long.

we looked for god in the
shadows flitting across the
faces of junkies who say fuck
the holy family with every
venous scar, in the hours spent
treated after beatings by Fort
Apache cops, in the church
with a priest who never says
a thing.

we looked for god going
hungry, unable to pay the
rent, write a sentence, find
work, wash away grief with
stupid lines like joy, love and
peace. we looked for god in
sleep, on the cheeks we kiss
on faces judged full of sin by
the people saying phony prayers.

we take turns now expecting
a divine word, though it appears

god has no time for wretched
spics who never dress slick for
church.

HOME

we have lived on this
street longer than the

women wearing their
covered heads, feeling

more than once the rosary
they pray cleansing us

for life in the flesh. we
have made the yearly

trip to Delancey Street
to find the Jewish store

with clothes to buy for
cheap to wear to Easter

Services to say we are
changed. just last week

we gathered at the little
creek by the water that

renewed Joseph for three
years and cleansed pretty

Rosa when her belly got
real big and felt morning

stars. we have lived in this
town waiting for years to

grow wings to fly among
the clouds with other dark

faces, experience whistling
wind and come a bit closer

to God's heavenly home.

THE TRUMP CRUSADE

I have watched events unfolding
for weeks waiting to hear a word

to comfort those who innocently
suffer like Christ without possibility

of resurrection, talking every night
with the stars that silently listen

to the terrible stories the migrants
share. I have watched the scattered

clouds roam overhead miraculously
carrying thousands of tears shed by

caged kids with carved crosses worn
around their necks, while trying my

very best to find strength to search
for sacramental bread, simple Masses,

and even thimble prayers from those
who claim to care in a world gone so

mad. I have listened to the words of
people fond of clicking their heels, felt

my heart dragged by a black Suburban
with politicians singing America the

beautiful in it, observed wingless Angels
move helplessly around shouting Spanish

names to white kin who sing the national
anthem without questioning what the future

will bring to this piece of geography called
by a colorful many home. without knowing

why I wait for truth to kick aside the mouths
full of loathing to make room for nobler voices

that will guide good people to undo
these dark hours before what remains

of America is a giant pile of ashes.

THE STONE

the last time I looked in the
alley there were clotheslines

stretched from wall to wall in
it, with cheap threads tightly

pinched by pins to them, and
faces looking out of windows

longing to be someplace other
than the South Bronx. I made

up stories about the dark shirts
like the one flapping like a flag

that belonged to Angel's father
in prison, the black shawls hung

to dry worn by the old woman in
love with church, the pretty blouses

worn by Jessica that she made look
handmade, and the occasional nasty

blond hair wig. I saw these things
almost daily wondering whether they

could pray or know anything about the
blocks exhausted gods, could they tell

me why the police batons beat Willy
long enough to make the buildings

scream and the little children screech
with tiring fear. on the way to public

school 66 each morning I would
glance at the alley aware the rest of

the city doesn't even know the people
who only own clotheslines live here,

then by the end of a week I would visit
the Saturday night confessional to tell

an Irish priest who just learned to speak
Spanish the damn stone where we live

is just never rolled away.

MIGRANT WOMAN

in the wrinkled black and white
photo she holds the Holy Book

with sweat streaming down her
earth colored brow. with dark

eyes in a slender migrant farmer
frame she hopes to break free. I

expect you know the fields that
consume her, the misty bleeding

landscape, the fretting hours spent
with others bent, the riches made

from her wounds, and the Spanish
tears she fetches from her most

intimate well. keep her divine
image in front of you, let the part

of you that is dead, stand beside
her with news that we are entirely

set free, rip out God's pages from
the book, request with fire in your

words the Holy keys, use them to
make the callous world tremble and

kiss for her sake the wicked dark
good-bye.

GENESIS

I remember playing on the
streets for hours and spinning

tops with friends who loved
staring at the flan displayed

in the Cuchifrito restaurant
window. together, we made

the long walk to a corner on
Southern Boulevard to buy

coquito that melted in our hot
hands, while we cracked jokes

impossible to tell at any other
time. we were the glad brown

boys of the South Bronx who
jumped on the bumpers of old

buses, swam in a dirty creek,
had water balloon fights, and

stayed up all night on Friday
listening to salsa on a twelve

transistor radio. we rode the
subway downtown making

big marks on trains to give
birth to graffiti that displayed

Spanish names, discovered white
America for the first-time ice skating

in a Central Park rink where we
fell with laughter, while an entire

set of new questions stirred inside.
I can only tell you now the world

began on the street with bewitching
sounds and tongues the rest of the

the city was hardly able to hear.

SIGNS

the hours spill into the
bright day to change you
on the cracked steps of
the Hoe Avenue church. they
can be counted on your weary
face, they gather like bodily Angels
crumbling things and urge you to
keep your sweet voice in a box
to hear it whisper in the dark
sugary things. this kind of day
never swings with shadows, it
waits with you for colorful flowers
to fall from the sky, then it enchants
your heart repeatedly with simple
signs of love.

MINUTIAE

the corner where all the buses
from Manhattan came to a stop,

greyed by exhaust fumes making
Jewish clerks in the candy store

cough profanities, still looks very
much like those days our feet ran

together. but the city has changed
over the years, more tenements have

fallen on harder times, the world is
closer to corruption, and the congas

that played in the little park no longer
take requests. young kids have quietly

grown old enough to take their turn
searching for a hint of hope in church

bells that ring in spite of the disbelief
in Saints, the Nazarene thought surely

dead, and all the talk about some God
who brings sustenance to the starving

souls on the block. the clock on Southern
Boulevard manages to go on blindly telling

time and in its own way reminding the
neighborhood newcomers who clumsily

roam in this intolerant country to keep
their colored faces one step ahead of

white dread and hate.

LONG ROAD

tell me Lord how many steps
will it take to carry this child

down the stony road to the
sound of the curving river?

do you mind lending me a little
light in the big dark so I can find

my way? tell me Lord when the time
comes can we jump on your shoulders

to make the crossing, will you mind
my infant's tears tumbling down your

cheeks, will your colored heart love us
in strange cities, will you learn English

with us, wash dishes, cut grass, empty
trash cans, clean toilets, mop floors, care

for white kids, build homes for the rich,
plant their flowers, harvest their crops,

and take an English name? tell me
Lord when will we sit face to face with

loved ones left on other lands, will the
Wall keep them out and us imprisoned,

will you be a homeless beggar like us?
tell me precious Lord, on the other side

of the Rio Grande will there be friends
who care, will you have look over us to

make certain our kids grow up free? go
on precious Lord speak, habla ya!

STORAGE

it is easy to disappear
in the storage room at
the edge of the big city
to see things in boxes
complimented by mere
dust. for months it has
become a reference space
to look at photos of the
child that held out a hand
to the parents who spoke
English like it dragged
them into the dark. in that
dimly lit place where you
ponder for hours the most
cherished pieces of the past
that memory cares to give,
you reminisce into the night,
alone. a lizard runs across
the floor, stops by your feet
to wink, and hurries away
through a crack that leads to

the Spring evening beyond
the storage chamber, and you
are convinced the fragile creature
is a shepherd leading you back
into the world. again, you put
away the photos, pack up the
recollections, and thank the old
man and lady expired for never
giving up—with longing inside
you exclaim Lord have mercy,
lock the door and march away
into the night.

STATE OF THE UNION

the state of the union
will be delivered to the

joint session of Congress
with the same filthy tongue

that spent months rehearsing
in public an avalanche of lies.

the world may even listen in for
a single fact, a smidgen of truth,

a statistic with pristine accuracy
to creep in front of the president's

eyes in language spelled with letters
easy enough for his simple mind. no

doubt there will be talk of border
walls to build, huddled masses from

shithole nations to rate more harm,
and America not taking another dark

child in. the sweet land of liberty will
be escorted once again down an unkind

road, further still from justice flowing
rivers, a long way from the mercy and

love that often inspired gracious ways.
tonight, the constitutionally mandated

address will try to sell us the idea we
have no alternative to the bigot in the

White House, the lover of white gowned
goons with a devil in their hearts, the keeper

of national illness, the speaker of hate
and supreme thief! yes, we might agree

this new American moment has more
costly torments yet to give! America,

America hurry light your lamps to
stay the expanding darkness!

I.C.E.

when they come for us at work,
in school, on the street, and in

our homes, what will you say?
when they snatch toddlers from

our brown arms, pat us down at
bus stops for speaking Spanish,

smash our faces with their clubs,
pound mothers' bodies with their

white fists, and make sure we are
noticeably dead, what will you say?

when they offer you their appalling
arguments to make dark skin turn the

color of blood, blow out candles in
church, turn away from the Galilean

Savior on the cross, and start to pile
bodies still drawing in what is left

of light at their for-profit immigration
detention centers, what will you say?

when we drop to our knees with white
society victims slung over our backs to

weep a sea of sadness, cradle what's
left of children who stare with wet

eyes in disbelief at hate, what will
you pray? when you see the long face

of the world with our eyes, will you
audaciously clear your loathing

throat to truthfully speak?

MORNING

spring morning begins with
the conspicuous perfume of

flowers in the air, a few stars
yet yawning, the light covers

used last night thrown aside, a
warming sun gently rising in

each heart, dingy faced bums
living on the streets showing

their smiles, mothers picturing
fairy tales to the sound of the

wind swept trees, sprinklers starting
their metronome dance over dry

grass, sanitized news in rolled
morning papers, bread lifted up

across the city in thanks, and a
quick look with a holy silence

at innermost thoughts cherished like
gracious bliss and unconditional

love.

MY FOSTER MOTHER

there is a time in the
course of life when you

see things on the coming
last goodbye the way they

were meant to be understood.
the hospital room where you

are surrounded by those
loved weeps as sickness

weakens you toward the reality
of dusty rest. your grown up

children read the bible verses
you love, beside you now they

empty their hearts of the words
you are to carry into the next world

where your body ravaged by illness
will find absolute rest. tonight, we

take your hand listening to you
whisper of recalled days beneath

a tree, walking at sunrise, wading
in Ohio rivers, giving birth, holding

grandchildren, and in church offering
small bundles of flowers in memory

of others. we have come to the hospital
room hoping for a little more life and

despite our sorrowing praying to a
God who waits for you. gently, you

begin to fade before our eyes, while
your blessed faith assures us there is

no dying of light!

GRAND CHILD

may I weep beside you on
this day your grandmother
died. may I say you will see
her in the years ahead in the
dark, the corridors at school,
crossing a street, at the table
in your home, in the stories
told, pictures shared, things
placed in boxes, and her voice
still whispering to her beloved
relations, keep on. on sleepless
nights made from blue feelings,
grandmother's gentle face will
look upon you and in all the
changing seasons her endless
love will find its way to you
on this side of the Cross.

COME SUNDAY

come Sunday after days
of weeping the familiar

worn out pew will try to
comfort us and the wait

for bread and wine will
seem not enough to make

up for the elderly woman
gone. we will exercise the

humble habit of speaking to
the Most High the words

gathered in a complex time
that left us with feelings of

godly abandonment. come
Sunday, we will sit in sacred

space recalling death from the
beginning of creation, like each

day the sun rises and goes down
over our heads, inherent in all

things. come Sunday, we will
try to start finding our dead in

the blowing wind, the rustling
leaves, the singing of birds, the

planted fields, the children in
loud play, a moon shimmering

above lake waters, and love that
remains in the dark. come Sunday,

we may even understand and grow to
love the words to everything there is

a season and a time for every purpose
under heaven.

THE KNOCK

I could hear the knocking on the door
with a knot in my throat that lasted

the entire night. from the fifth floor
window to the filthy old street, I looked

at others roaming around who had known
the block since childhood now carrying

small brown paper bags hiding the beer
cans they raised to their lips to wash away

the misery lingering from broken dreams.
each day we purchase life with sorrow

running from la Migra and whispering
beneath exhausted breath words to the

great Silence that left us to live beyond
hope in this new hell-on-earth. we have

walked with God for longer than anyone
can recall, inhaled incense in sanctuaries

from Spanish squares to English streets,
smiled when the northern sky gave signs

of divine light, draped ourselves in the
fond memories of escaped distant homes,

felt solace smelling the ancient earth and
wondered why the land of milk and honey

is still fucken far away. the holy Chariot
with freedom wheels cannot find us, the

voices on the mountain-top never seem to
say our names and America the beautiful

hands us her best hanging rope and slave
chains.

THE ODOR

the strong odor fell on the
neighborhood catching

everyone's attention, like
those days when bodies

festered next to coffee trees
beneath the hot sun, with

Spanish vultures circling
above them, and old women

kneeling near them to talk
them into heaven. on the block

those wounded by empire smiled
in spite of it in the bent hours of

long days, bought flowers from
Southern Boulevard to place in

the middle of the kitchen table
to sweeten up the stench, placed

tiny pieces of paper with petitions
in water beneath a stone on altars

with their favorite saint, and tried
never to think of the second-rate

compass directing their lives. in
the thick sleepy night the scent crept

into dreams raising in them walls to
high for Jacob's ladder on earth and

they ran along its base endlessly in
search of a door. deeper into the night

in their crowded rooms they cried
out in sleep, obscenely afraid of what

another day intolerant of the rancid odor
would bring and eager to take refuge in

tiny crosses worn around their detested
brown necks.

THE SCRAPS

the tiny room with paint
blistering on the wall had
a window that opened
alone as if inviting pigeons
on windy nights to come in.
she would get up at night to
push it back down, then sit
on a torn chair unable to sleep
thinking of the day to come, God
weeping for the unschooled in love,
how loud to shout for heaven to hear,
and what to say to people who saw
in her brown face an unwelcomed
alien. the flowers in the room
slowly opened on an altar trembling
when she prayed about troubled days.
her questions were never answered by
the ceramic Saint she dusted, the sickly
pews at church that were out of touch with
the good news of the executed Nazarene
and the robed religious men who only

lifted the hem of their robes to step over
her never changed it seemed by the wafers
on their Holy tables. in the dark room, the
women imagined the One called living
bread would one day knock on her door
to grant the wishes she longed dreamed.

MORNING

the morning comes with
light falling from the sky
like gentle rain. I hear the
sound of footsteps in the
hallway making their way
down the tenement steps,
heading out into the city
for another slogging day
of work downtown, that
always follows after the
Spanish morning prayer,
to which Sparrows perched
on the chilly window ledges
are drawn. incense burning
in someone's apartment has
entered my room beneath
the crack of the front door
giddily making its rounds
in the space encouraging
dawdling thoughts for those
in it with me. I deeply breath

its fragrance aware it is burning
down on Margaritas' bedroom
altar for everyone within its
conspicuous reach, then I close
my eyes dreaming the voices
coming to life around me might
today give God in heaven a big
surprise—then, totally awake
I sink into the space of a new
day in this city seething with
life!

ANOTHER

after another school shooting
horror again swells sorrowing

hearts faster than any can say
Jesus' name, more innocent

blood ran the halls in Florida on
Ash Wednesday to make the nation

fall into exhumed darkness, the
speechless religious leaders shiver

into bits, and the naïve politicians
weep. we kneel now only to beg the

Lord to help us pray on this terrifying
last day, to lift words so often said

in the recurring nightmare and break
remembrance bread that has yet to

deliver comfort, life and peace for those
left by their beloved now dead. people

on every shore around the globe join the
wailing, churches are filled to the rafters

with tears, and not one hymn or steeple
filled with resonant prayer can lift the

cup of life to our lips. tell us explainers
of heavenly things for the sake of children

and the lost when will evil walk into the
fiery lake, and disappear?

THE FIRE HYDRANT

the fire hydrant in the middle
of the block was opened so
kids lingered tossing popsicle
sticks in the water streams it made
against the edges of the sidewalk.
on that day a tiny cross floated up
from who knows where, it made its
way passed the bodega, the barber
shop, the beauty salon, the Catholic
thrift store, and people on the stoops
who did not understand the first thing
about it. even though I was one of the
kids playing around I reached into the
water to pick it up and without saying
a thing, carried it across the street to
the building we lived in and put the thing
on the top ledge of our front door frame
in case it could do something for tough
days. I rushed back to the music of the
open pump imagining the sounds it made

and the laughter around it full of secrecy
for our street, then I put my arms around
my slaughter house brother and friends
to say I love you bros.

THE CITY

my days are the city sitting
on the stoop in the dim light
of early Spring evening, the

apartments all emptied of
residents, Spanglish tongues
unzipped, children running

the sidewalks pointing to the
two lights on the number two
subway speeding the curve

on the tracks at a distance,
and closing my eyes to listen
to the voices of dead friends

who tell me they are present
in the warm breeze that softly
brushes my face. some days

when I peel back sadness, I
close my eyes and see the old
women who took Sunday night

walks with the nuns, the elderly
men who drank beer wearing caps
with the names of the wars that

made them Vets, ambulance lights
lighting up the street like it was
Christmas, cats crawling beneath

parked cars and the pigeons that
found thousands of ways to call us
to other haunts. my days are the

city filled with beggars, junkies,
winos, sinners and saints looking
for the slightest sign of a world

worthy and without end.

REFUGEE

the rain comes to the window
all day long with a tiny finger

gently tapping messages from
the refugees living in the other

building from the country some
were shot for carrying a picture

of a priest, coffee bean pickers
who never went to school, boys

forced to be soldiers and girls
who were beaten and raped.

the wind is blowing hard enough
to carry the sounds of crying

they toss into the alley from
broken English tongues, the

curses flung at pain inflicting
gods, and a nation that will not

give compassion for their dark
colored kind. not a single spot is

dry outside, the pools on the sidewalk
grow by the second, the night is wet

and without stars, the refugees' words
across the alley faintly take shape in

in our heads and we hear them saying
once we had a home in paradise though

death was scattered in the fields, but
here we are unwelcomed, stomped and

jailed by men of might for the wrong
life.

WELCOME

in this country far from us
that others settled with big

dreams, crowned their days
with liberty, vowed to crush

old tyrants and equality to
breathe, we have come in

waves with loads unbearable
to speak, chains still rattling on

our limbs, and told by tickled
pink lips we don't believe your

sobbing! each day that slowly
passes, what we have is taken in

fields that soak our blood, the
factories that age us, the fast

food grills that pay us with little
more than dirt, the buildings we

conspicuously clean, and children
soaked in privilege who parents

expect our calloused hands to hold
with tenderness and keep. some

day their reflection will be seen in
the black of our eyes, a million wild

flowers will fall from the sky, the
dry mouths will once again sweet-talk

America to begin, cheap gods will be left
to perish, they will take us by our brown

hands, chase away flies hurrying to nest
on our graves, find strength to say foreign

sounding names, then summon the word
welcome to their abusive white lips.

SHOTS FIRED

schools are paced by troubled
boys with a whole arsenal of

guns longing to deliver death
to their peers and grief to the

living. the mounting bodies and
those made to join the pile of

ruin tomorrow have no need of
vacant prayers, hollow empathy

from paid for politicians, and high
sounding words about yet more

plans to do nothing.　how long
must we sob in the unimaginable

dark and shout to the Holy Mother
of God tales of mortal butchery in

places of learning made to lacerate
flesh?   weeping, weeping without

end, the funeral homes are filled with
the frames of the young and dearly

adored, flattened by a wickedness
mocking heaven and the legislators

who go out of their way to keep them
bullet dead. do prayers have any truth

to tell? do the halls of Congress
feel the crippling pain? Does God?

FRIDAY

the lengthy day turned a
corner to wind down again

in the apartment crowded
like a thieves' den on the

other side of the street, far
from the church's clatter,

the sanctimonious neighbors,
and the police cars riding the

streets God does not deliver
from sin. in these evening

hours women in the apartment
find they are absorbed with garish

thoughts about hopeful things,
while music plays loud for the

kids with them who practice
dance steps. the cramped living

room is like a faceless creature,
waiting to catch a simple feel

of warm light and plain old
fantastical peace. I heard love

bursting from a throat in the
kitchen that said Friday night

fish is ready. the empty stomachs
carried to the kitchen were filled

that night with equal grades of
joy—the miracle of bread and

Spanglish talking around a thrift
shop table . . . que cosa!

THE STONE

walking on slippery streets
with a few leaves blown to

rest at your feet, sometimes
stopping to say a prayer in

places of grief, kneeling in
front of the Mural of Big Pun

on a building with decaying
bricks, the wall people visit to

hear speak, taking pleasure in
the sounds of children at play,

the gentle smiles of the widows
sitting on the stoops, catching an

occasional glimpse of Angels
from heaven escorting the cold

dark to a distant place, not a
finger on the hand of hostile

time has reach. you think of
the world that does not know

this block, the mothers fainting
in church when mass is said for

another dead kid, the same fine
air we breathe with the uptown

white crowd in beautiful brown
skin, the dreams prancing about

at night beneath the stars offering
light, and tell yourself someday

the blood-soaked stones on the
block will speak.

SIMPLE

when the day light is about
gone, the wind has changed

direction, and the sound of
keys turn in the old apartment

doors, the feel of a new life
gives us pleasure even in the

smallest of things. we look
into the distance from Bronx

rooftops with the sounds of
Orquesta Harlow thundering

over the streets, counting off
the curses left in the bloody

fields, the faces of whimpering
missionaries, the decrepit hours

in church listening to sermons
pretending America's empire

is the New Jerusalem. together,
without a word talked in dragging

night, we search for a different
Eden, even if it means endlessly

living in aging tenements crying
for Jesus. we will keep on dreaming

of things like hidden pearls and
the good life on the edge of words

that one day will speak loudly on
the corners of our half-welcoming

world!

TELL ME

when I heard them say with
knife sharp words you don't

belong, sitting on the eroded
steeps of a Spanish speaking

stoop, the silhouette of the
buildings downtown kept clean

by our mothers from the block
visible in the distance, the noisy

hate edging into our born in the
U.S.A. brown hearts, it was clear

the chains were not gone, and a
thousand seasons of dreaming on

these shores were again forsaking
us. in the apartments, we awake

screaming in the middle of night,
make up prayers just to startle the

dark, question when and where the
great Will begins, and wonder what

ever happened to the truth with eyes
like a burning furnace and hands that

swing doors open? someone, anyone
on this land, pray tell!

EL NORTE

there are no mountains rising at
the edge of city streets, no mythical

birds circling the rooftops, no
Mayan temples reaching for the

heavens, no soldiers on foot to
shoot us on the stoops, no forest

to mute the screams of priests who
search for youth long disappeared.

instead, in the North, we sling the
coffee offloaded at docks straight

from the bloody Central American
fields, peasant families see their kids

drown in tears, learn to saturate their
tongues with drink and dress in rags

from thrift shops to go to school,
church and work. at night, ancient

spirits tell us tales, elders with
thick memories from shores they

named keep us on the edges
of second-hand chairs and we

imagine God on the block might
come soon to complete a bloody

divine mission.

THE MISSION

the mission house was dimly
lit, the worn sheets on the bunks

smelled of mold, a small office
beside the front door served as the

staff interview room, where the tired
homeless sat to tell their stories like

strangers on the Road to Emmaus
removing masks to show themselves

human beings with full names. the
junkies, drunks, and discarded kids

who frequently visited the place for
food to put in their stomach and shelter

from the blasphemies of good Christian
neighbors, dropped into anonymity again

and again, after evening prayer. on the
top bunk an old wino talked about his

life like it was an express train rushing
into a dark tunnel, a young boy on another

bunk choked on his tears, a member of
the staff walked by to announce lights

out in ten, and everyone in the dormitory
looked around like they were desperately

trying to find signs of hope for a good night
of sleep.

GOOD FRIDAY

after marking bible pages with
ink for years on the rooftop,

spending Friday nights lost
kissing the bottle pouring cheap

wine down his throat to make
new words, even sprouting legs

some times to travel the Lower
East Side streets, he would lay

down allowing his mind to travel
back years to innermost places

rarely shown to others. his deepest
questions lived in the whispering

apartments, in the junkie children
birthed, the hard-working Spanish

speaking poor, the new Americans
waiting in their mother's wombs

to exit, the Puerto Rican priests,
Irish nuns, the school custodians,

and the living who go missing each
day in the hearts of people better off.

sometimes, he would stand at the
rooftop edge to stare at the East

River way older than Carmen's
first born, making up words to

describe the bad taste pious talk
left in the mouths of his Good

Friday people.

THE VISIT

I remember the first day
in the apartment with three

unfurnished rooms, an old
mattress on a bedroom floor,

and a kitchen table with two
chairs. by then Shorty had

departed the junkie world
with fifteen puncture wounds

across his chest, the price for
a ten-dollar bag of dope and

not one candle flaming in the
pretty church could bring him

back. I listened to the voices
of a brother and close friend

living in that hole, not once touched
by churchly prayer, called by name

to an early grave, leaving the rest
of us on the block with homeless

love. I wondered what would become
of other faultless kids and thought

staring at the lifeless bodies in coffins
at the Ortiz Funeral Home why the pretty

words preached at St. John's Church
failed, always. then, I had to confess

the much talked about resurrected Jesus
must have gotten lost on the way to the

South Bronx.

SUNDAY

the mailman never handed me
a letter on the corner, there was

no mother able to see into the
future, no father praying on his

knees for divine power to save
us, no needle to penetrate a

vein deep enough to help me
overcome a world that ate us

like acid on flesh. I told my life
story to the walls in cheap hotel

rooms rented to kids, wept for the
day a welcome mat would be thrown

on the floor of the apartment door,
came out of junkie nods waiting to

hear God speak louder than cops,
laughed myself to sleep many nights

in the old tenement alley wrapped with
cardboard boxes thinking of a porcelain

Jesus in pretty churches. I stumbled
homeless for years on city streets, grew

tired by the hour of my own tears, and
saw the coming and going of too many

young lives. midway to nowhere, I did
my best to eavesdrop on the promises of

heaven I was certain longed to speak in
the language of my imagined Eden for

the fucked-up world skinning people
alive on the streets!

THE CHALICE

it's another Sunday for
wandering off to church
by walking poorly cleaned
streets where heaven in tiny
blades of grass pushes through
sidewalk cracks and gathered
congregants find divinity in
the appointed hour. my junkie
friends sit in the first pew oblivious
to curses hurled at them, talking about
the dope sucking up their souls and
situations that scare them. the priest
takes the stage like Prometheus about
to give us all a gift, inviting us to lean
closer to his words, open our blood shot
eyes and see the veil of darkness being
peeled away. people in the sanctuary
looking around want so badly to bend
their knees in adoration and give up the
toil of their worlds for the beautiful sake
of the truth heard and the foolish drink
inside the altar chalice.

THE DREAM

I dreamed of knocking on
a door last night that had a

sign from which pamphlets
floated up with chattering

words about no more room
for travelers with dark colored

skin in schools, homes, shops,
and streets in the great North

where rivers find hundreds of
ways to weep. I felt sickness

like a gust of wind keeping the
door shut from the other side,

but had no desire to leave and
continued only pounding a bit

harder, the fingers on my hand
slackening with blisters, after

several weeks standing in front
of the door and whispering the

sorrows of Spanish speaking lands
eagerly purchased by America's

White House with the flick of
a pen, I knelled in the darkness

thinking God surely must be able
to hear my prayers.

THE LUNCH HOUR

it was the middle of the day
with people streaming into

the food court to gossip like
grandmothers in a poorly lit

marketplace. hanging on every
word the young pale faced man

listened to a tight-lipped mouth
with a lust for blood sound the

alarm on Mexican day laborers
in the name of a monstrous God

that collars brown necks until they
are thrown across the border. at

another table, a graying couple spoke
with hearts made of Sundays that never

exhale a word of judgement, and it
was apparent pieces of the Last Supper

were in their Black hands. several
brown faces speaking Spanish took

a seat beside them folding Pizza, gave
thanks for the dark hands that made it,

and added their warmth and light
to the room to chase away monstrous

shadows. at the end of the gossip hour,
the nearly hidden sacred came upon

us in this astonishing way!

IMPENITENT

the holier than thou loved
to say nothing of the goose

stepper in the white house
spending his evenings coming

up with new ways to startle
blood in those once slaves and

now beaten of life each day
for having dark skin. dirty

evenings parade in our tax
paid rooms, just across from

a park where homeless vets,
undocumented mothers, and

homeless roaming kids drench
the tired wide space with fresh

tears. the sorrow on the streets
falls into place just beyond the

unkind man's gates, the capital
house inches closer to the dark

side of the moon and voices to
raise from oblivion the dead just

whisper their horror about hate
closing borders, limiting dissent,

and with utter mockery weighing
down democracy with big stones

for deep lakes. from the rubbish
heap beating in his chest, the sickly

words thrown from his lips, we confess
the lynched carpenter will have the last

word in the sure to come black hearse
ride that will deliver impenitent old

men to a proper hell.

CARRY US

already the people speak
of the simple things the

clocks sound by the hour to
inch them closer to messages

of colorful life. on the corner
children look in each direction

beneath a deep spreading sky
and at places sadness cannot

ever reach. the simple truth is
divinity loves the candle-lights

slowly burning in these lives that
step each day on the savage ground

of Golgotha. grandmothers who gather
on the sidewalk for talk feed on odd

thoughts like time is a miracle sent
to tease battered years. the mumbling

below heaven is a bit loud in the
secluded apartments far from the

bony churches where our mouths
labor to tell the rest of the world

where it hurts. at midnight, when
the masks are stripped, we cry out

for a simple look at the mystery
that whispers alleluias in our big

hearts.

THE CLOSING

we stand on the corner
waiting once again for

Christ's Easter flinching
at the words coming out

of a television set in Joey's
barber shop. the angry White

president just said the day
is coming when it will be

necessary to close the border
for a time. with the dirty habits

of hate, this absurd politician sees
a nation with policed boundaries,

the dark skin expelled and adversarial
citizens carefully choked to death.

reason has yet to make a home inside
the president's senior citizen head

that finds a thousand different ways
to canorously belch the imprudent

foul beliefs that make us sink, and
weep. what voice from the great

American dream fades now from sea
to sea?   who believes closed doors

will really make and keep us safe
and free? How long will crafters

of callous policy and law follow
the man writing backwards and

lost? who will see foreigners
like human beings and treat

them like equals on this piece
of American earth?

THE TAKE OVER

buildings open their mouths this
morning to swallow dizzy news

carried by thick sentences tossed
to the world from a big face. you

see people hurrying along the street
rushing to work where they sell the

skin on their bones, while the incurable
mad billionaire elected by fear devours

them with bitterness. we listen
wondering how in the world these

demented politicians managed their
way into office though choirs in the

distance mourned? the boot lickers
these days appear to wait for the Last

Supper to end so they can have a dance
around the killing trees with their own

Judas whispering there is no God but
me! even the ancient dead are crying

in their graves—how long sweet
Lord? How long sweet Lord until

heaven and earth return to Martin's
brilliant dream? a young boy walks

pass in a wrinkled shirt on his way to
trembling pews where Spanish speakers

gather to call on divine grace to end
the disabling darkness—we pray!

THE KNOCK

dear Mr. Laboda we sent the
children to your school today
despite being told the knock
on the door is only a few hours
away. they were up all night
with me in the living room
listening to the noise on the
street, the bullets that began
reporting, the wino talking out
loud about nasty things, and I
saw mothers gathered for prayer
on the corner where little Papo
was found dead. yesterday, the
storefront preacher convinced us
the resurrection time would come
with the fresh morning so we all
dreamt joy. the kids may be a
little tired today in your classroom
and disappointed that the promise
God seems to have taken a walk on
another block, which seems to have

left him too exhausted to deliver paradise to our door. do what you can to teach them how to get out of this cage until deliverance comes for them.

LOCK UP

every morning before leaving
the apartment for school the

little boy imagined talking with
his father in jail. he complained

about the trousers turning into
puddle jumpers by the week and

thought they could be taken to a
dry cleaner to let the cuffs down

before his father was set free. every
week he wore those slacks to P.S. 66

using them to chart his growth and
the time separated from his father

who was locked up for standing next
to a bag of dope one Sunday on the

block that wasn't even his. when
Parents' Day came up at the school

he sat quietly in the classroom and
handed the teacher a note from his

father that he carefully composed that
said unfortunately work prevents him

from attending. at the end of the school
day, he would return to his fifth floor

apartment to unpack a picture of his
old man, explain he grew a bit taller

and then press together another
simple letter to explain with more

pious lies why his jailed Papi never
visited the school.

LOOK

I reached the bridge stretched
across the river when the clock

on the village square began to
bellow, the rushing water below

me carrying tears out to the far
sea, and the Cathedral with the

painted wall of the Last Supper
attended by smiling peasants

ringing her bells. I have walked
that bridge many times to watch

the night lifted by northern winds
to the shimmering stars, rested in

the middle to recite loudly the old
tales of mythical creatures of the

dark the widows loved to tell the
kids in their charge, and when the

last crosser wandered away I stared
at the dying river wondering with

her where home truly lays. then,
I looked at the narrow river-banks

for signs of life, the homeless the
church pities, the undocumented

children in mothers' arms barely
hidden from sight, and recalled

stories of love, paradise, kindness
and grace that questioned misery

without end.

GRADUATION

you have all walked across
the stage with dreams to stand

before us with robes, speeches,
joys, quandaries, and whispering

lips about completion. you who
cradled books long into the next

morning, with butterflies turning
inside your stomachs to the very

end, take the last flight with all
your labors worn brightly on your

festive faces. gone are the days you
nearly believed it could not be done,

the nights of tackling study with new
tears and the feeling of having nothing

left to give. today, we celebrate your
wise becoming on the stage, the ways

you know the leaves of a flowering
tree of knowledge and the light you

share with us. today, you depart on
roads leading to other harvests and

these halls, scholars and dear precious
friends in light and dark will always

be near.

ANIMALS

who speaks for the faceless
strangers searching for bread,

begging for life and hideously
named?   who believes the divinity

come from heaven above is made
of beautiful dark skin, the wretched

refuse of the earth, the objects of
a pale faced leader's destructive

urge, the blameless lined up daily
for death? who has eyes to see rejected

human beings set on high hills, nailed
callously to trees like the jobless carpenter

who shrieked? I hear religious books
have thousands of wise words that have

crawled for too many years and talked
in different tongues to help us find our

way. I hear the White House studies
one of them each week, abusing firm

truth, prowling hellish darkness, and
explaining hate for good! America,

America, crucified people come to
show scarred bodies, dreams and

words—what makes you blind and
deaf?

SANTA FE SHOOTING

at Santa Fe High School, floors
are mopped of blood, after yet

another shooting has left many
drenched with tears. we know

the scene by heart, the uncountable
bullets that have led many to their

grave, the weeks of debate that
will never respond completely to

the names of these new dead and
the politics that keeps lowering new

coffins into graves. today, a young
boy with monstrous dreams fired

a perfectly scaled gun into warm
bodies and delivered from dark depths

an eternal silence that will never tire
of grabbing us by the neck nor mocking

prayers raised to heaven, everywhere. our
sorrow blows like ash across this earth,

shaky hope is darkened by unbearable
feelings of a country lost and the good

news again goes into hiding. when will
this long night end, the cowering under

tables stop, the mass murder lesson plans
from Columbine, Sandy Hook, Parkland,

Santa Fe and too many others see a
hellish fate? How many moments of

silence is needed for action against
such despair dealing violence?

ANOTHER WEEPING

the moon has come out
on a warm night where
trees rattle leaves at the
spot the road ends with
bad news. we will sit
for a little while pushed
into silence on the turning
earth, trying to measure
the weight of years that
persevered without a hint
of light, wondering about
the children who tremble in
schools, and how the paradise
may have been no more than
a foolish dream. the places
where blood was spilled follow
us with the faces of those long
passed returning, we wipe our
eyes of tears and prepare to hear
in the new morning the mournful
ringing of the city's old Cathedral
bells!

THE SPEAKING TREE

the speaking tree in the
middle of the city ripens

800 languages on brown
limbs and loves to tell us

in Spanish how to catch
the train on Christopher

Street. the trunk is tall
with names carved out in

other tongues and it has
even learned to call out

a few old English names
found deep within those

old tenements that slowly
have changed. the speaking

tree in my mother tongue does
wonder about some uptown

white homes that cannot get
along without Spanish cleaning

ladies, brown arms that press
their clothes, dark hands that

love their kids, and hate that
makes them feel big. the speaking

tree loves the clamorous voices,
the after-hour noises, the block

to block salsa the unkind will
never dream and the foreign

God who made it with gentle
puffs of breath. the speaking

tree tells our black and brown
faced kids come sit with me y

contemos las estrellas—even
now they sit with the speaking

tree filling their Spanish hearts
with glorious counted stars!

THE CURE

down by the east river
the birds still sing in the
early morning, the current
can be seen by the naked
eye and you easily fall in
love with mysteries that
cast away the commotions
of the rest of the world. the
names written on stone for
your thoughts fall into the
rising light and those who
detest Jose, Milagros, Maria
and Angel have no admission
here. today, this place feels
like first love offering sweet
peace, the hereafter entering
your lungs and you will return
to your single room flat with a
cure for sadness.

THE SUBWAY RIDE

we slept like strangers on
the subway surrounded by

children with loose teeth and
old men reading salacious tales

in The Daily News. we rode the
subway across three boroughs

with our things fitting into two
worn pockets, glad to be a step

ahead of the darkness of Silver
Mont graves, beyond the arms

that held us and told us stories
before bed. I kept three books

in a brown bag about hobbits,
that frequently invited me to

come with them, imagine heaven
near, the temptations that could

never win, evil cast to the flames,
and faces in the metal monster

that glare escaped. the riders
had places to be, people to dine

with, and homes for sleep, we
rode the steel box in smelly clothes,

instead. we listened one night to a
young man who boarded the train

at 149th street with an old guitar,
he pulled from the case a small

bottle of Holy Water that he
sprinkled in the clanging car,

and then began to sing about
the world's blanket of shame.

man, this was street music from
the sweet Lord who promised

good for us!

A CLEAR DAY

the people on this block
cannot be translated into

library books written by
Midwesterners who just

came to town. our hopes,
struggles, Spanish thoughts

and dreams cannot simply be
captured by mere academic

skills and deceits. we utter in
the storefront church, la bodega,

the places of work, schools, and
the cages we ache under lock

and key our heart-deep secrets
beneath brown skin. we laugh, weep

and live in ways to turn white
faces red, without masks to hide

our curious souls, and with half
frightened looks about who now

comes to take us away. come see
for yourself the way the moon

shines in our eyes, the way we
hold each other in love, how we

crown children with dreams, and
you will admit somebody has yet

to write correctly of us.

NEW WORLD

when the sun was bright over
the rooftops, we landed here
after walking for miles to risk
new visions. we made room
for optimism on the long journey
and felt teased by thirst for this
new world. we broke loose from
the centuries old chains Spaniards
placed on our wrists that gave us
pain greater than drowning at sea.
we came to breathe free, to find the
good Lord smiling on the streets, to
have our children grow up to write
epics about thousands of displeasures
left behind, the earth that bled and
a north country promising not to bury
them alive. we came here like strangers
called home invited to forget the open
eyes of the dead left far away and the
lonely hearts that have kept us distant
from Eden. we came to the city crowded

with many tongues, the world with many
churches talking of love, surviving the
saddest histories of hate and finally in
all the world to this place we endlessly
shall call home!

THE TABLE

I made custom jewelry
for hours. Tito Puente
played timbales on the
record player just for
us. we helped a teen
mother make money
with smiles on a cold
South Bronx day. I
strayed around the
apartment for bouts
of rest, looked into the
darkness singing dirty
songs about the street and
thanked God for pausing
at the table in our worn
out old world.

THE WRECKAGE

just below the window
visible from the street

Henry painted a big H
to exhibit for years on

the block. the letter that
registered his weight on

earth grew old with him
in the neighborhood until

he turned to dust and the
shred of his name on the

building too was laid to
waste for a condo. we can

remember the day rubble
was left behind on the old

tenement lot, the cold night
it was arsoned by kids, the

days of standing across the
street wondering in cold air

how long it would be until
the whole barrio was made

wreckage. we saw the street
slowly taken over by machines,

the local Cathedral become less
populated by people, stores

on the boulevard not speaking
Spanish and the White people

of money who had no time
to stoop for a glimpse at the

mystery of God in brown
faces, increase. whatever

happened to the people run
over by property lines, the poor

families who lost their homes,
the kids who were carried north,

and mothers' who rode the subway
for work downtown? Whatever

happened to the Black and Brown
poor who have a right to live?

WAITING

I cannot begin to tell
you how many drunken

gravediggers have wiped
sweat from their brows

in cemeteries where school
age friends are distributed.

just today I would like to
see the Crucified carpenter

witnesses say arose from
the dead come stroll along

on these real-world fields
to yell at him is this the love

you mean. I cannot begin to tell
you of the endless bitterness

mothers who prayed felt
lowering kids who barely

lived into the everlastingly
silent pit. today I want to look

into that resurrected face to
spit up a wad of indecorous

words about never forgetting
the young boys and girls who

left this world before their time
without a holy visit. I cannot

begin to tell you about our poor
schools, crowded rooms, frayed

clothes, pathetic wages and under
class status in the land of the free.

someday, I hope Lord you
make me take back what

my tongue daily curses, but
right now where the fuck

are you?

THE WAIT

at the bus stop a cat slid
across the cobble stone

street for people who
practiced patience that

morning and talked in
Spanish about last nights

bad dreams. they make
these rounds every day

of the week going over
things in their heads, a

few holding children by
the hand, until they make

the old bus stop and
their kids walk away to

school. a young mother
with an infant in her arms

looks at other eyes for new
signs of life, then whispers

in the baby's tiny ear this
beats the merciless walk

across three borders, mija.
the passengers stand quietly

but you can almost hear the
language of hopefulness that

rattles in their heads and
the love they bring to a new

home far from dictator's flags
raging in the wind.

THE VETERAN

I walked the supermarket
aisles this afternoon seeing

Tito arranging mangoes in
the fruit section talking to

them like they were still
hanging on a tree. I passed

him like a store detective
noticing the prosthetic leg

just below his knee always
reminding him of a tour in

the middle east. Tito tells
stories in the neighborhood

with his limp and sits early
in the evening on the stoop to

recite tales he carries like
precious gems. sometimes

he happens to mention pieces
of what he confessed to the

priest who listens to more
than he cares to hear, often

Tito is just alone crying and
disappearing in his thrift store

clothes. pious about freedom
learned from school books, hated

in his country for having dark
skin, Tito clenches his fists at

the muddled nation in love with
drinking the blood of people like

him.

SIMPLE MATTERS

the old man loved to catch
the simple talk of the kids

who stayed up all night hanging
on the street until the last stars

withdrew from the sky. the sweet
scent of a new day, the soft light

of the warming sun and the fresh
morning waking from last night's

shadows always aroused in him
untroubled feelings only known

by the gods. it did not matter that
his Salvadoran mind had slowed

or that tears poured on his bed
from memories spilled from a

crinkling heart, especially when
intoxicating joy was blown by the

wind to him on walks. in his weak
hand, he carried a copy of a Spanish

newspaper for company on the bench
in the little park to read news about the

side of town that masked matters of
truth. he laughed at the formulas for

poverty reportedly shared by the best
minds that never physically touched

a poor hand attached to faces deemed
unwelcome in a nation led by cruel

rich old men.

LOISAIDA

on the Lower East Side
along Avenue D where

bibles gather dust in the
projects and scribbling

on tenement walls tell
stories about dead boys

with beautiful black and
brown skin, the people

wait for words to bring
them light and any god

having no other place to
be. we gave a name to

everything, rebirthed the
city streets in Spanglish,

backed a Nuyorican actor
and tiny church pastor on

a community board to push
a vote to retitle Avenue C

with a name first said by
Abuelita lips—Loisaida!

nowadays, our eyes never
run out of water when we

look up to see a street sign
that reads Loisaida Avenue

reproving the invisibility of
people like us. before the

sun sets on the last day of
the new year, children all

grown up will write a library
of poems about sofrito people

who long for a welcoming new
world.

CRIMINALIZED

my crime in this nation of
immigrants was to cross the

border without permission,
to display my fresh wounds,

escape my chains and masters'
whips and foolishly seek mercy

in English settlers' depths. I can
shorten my name, work three

jobs, live the inner city, speak
English like a crown prince,

raise kids to be good citizens, then
expect to hang on a tree. I came

from the place that made America
wealthy, I carry the voices of the

orphaned, tortured and dead, the
memories of those who gasp for

air, the human beings called animals
by white fear and know too well

the putrid excrement flung on these
shores at strangers like us. my crime

in the thin atmosphere of this ailing
nation is to have the wrong colored

skin, name and tongue.

AWAKE

in the morning light, with
eyes widening in watch,
we sit quietly trying once
more to solve the mystery.
the rich, poor, black, white,
red, yellow and brown in the
world at large must know before
death how eternity steps in to
separate the dust. in restless strife
with returning questions about
the sublime flow of life, with the
same heart that beats in every chest,
below the hills where lilies bloom,
we search for certainty, the Holy with
true depth, the thing that sets us free
to sing: O death where is thy sting?
Grave, thy victory?

THORNS

the national guard has taken up
positions at the border with little

power to do anything against the
mostly women and children with

mustard seed hearts in fearful
flight. the new political theater

reeks like a sack of shit tossed on
the national stage to be approved

by the White House theologians,
intellectuals fond of their vilifying

lips, philosophers undaunted by
the wretched of the earth and

too many elected officials kissing
the pale face ass of a billionaire

pretending to be president of a
nation that once grieved for the

destitute at its door. a fortune in
taxes are spent to label strangers a

threat, to criminalize their skin and
demonize their tongue, and ready

them for indecorous graves. thank God
they are brave enough to come to speak

to citizens about the murder of history,
to gather for prayer on corners and declare

with broken English the meaning of the
good news on which all the president's

men relieve themselves.

MOTHER TONGUE

you could keep silent all
day cursing in Spanish in
your head while working

your skin to the bone on the
white side of town. you
might go unnoticed in the

darkness, forget about your
colored God, wake up each
morning confused about what

to do with your children, kneel
at night before your bedroom
altar and not find a single word

resting on your tongue to offer
Jesus and the saints. you could
spend the next month learning

to read the toxic signs saying
English only, turning your back
on them after understanding and

taking the hand of the refugee
mother in the apartment next
door until you reach the little

church offering legal aid to people
like her, again without speaking a
single word. you could allow the

silence to creep in around the edges
of your eyes like water from the
big English-speaking Hudson River,

then drown you with foreign words
or you could finally draw a line on
the sidewalk dividing living things from

the dead and spend long days shouting
in the public square your good enough
Spanish thoughts!

THE AGE TO COME

the old man living on the
first floor in our tenement
dragged his flesh around the
neighborhood stopping on
the stoops to tell gathered kids
timeless stories spoken on the
verge of tears about youth a
little more gone. pointing to the
subway station in the distance,
he said that is where sixty years
earlier he saw the cloudy flat
sky of the Bronx, then moved
into the corner building, drank
his first cup of light beer and watched
on the rooftop with his mother quiet
in a beach chair the night sky come
to life on Independence Day. with
ghastly details he talked about the
service rendered in southeast Asia,
the extraordinary look in the eyes
of forgotten vets wasted in basements

like junkie men and the old country
in the middle of the vast sea among
the first to speak the geography of
Europe changed. in his eyes you
could see the little child grown old
still searching for the perfect broken
English dream.

LOST BOYS

we walked the Grand Concourse
one darkening night recalling the

flowers in the small pot in bloom
left on the kitchen table beside a

mother immeasurably lost by the
delivery of a high sentence to her

two boys. our heartbeats were
loud enough to hear on Walton

Avenue where we hoisted heavy
loads inside our heads and dope

ran freely in our veins. we pounded
restaurant doors for food, slept on

abandoned building floors and
were turned away by people who

loved to bury Christ in brand new
bibles. we were the street kids of

the South Bronx rejected by everyone,
slaughtered by neglect, drugs and

guns, eating from trash cans, trading
our bodies for a dime, in the same

clothes for days without end, doing
time for stealing bread, writing long

messages on walls to God and waiting
in vain for the Savior who forgot to

count among his saving cost a little
time to think of us.

FLOWERS

in the corner building
a young girl comes out
in her first communion
white dress purchased
in a Jewish store on far
away Delancey street.
her brown face smiles
without worry as if to
say to the world not one
dream for her will ever
be broken. she will tell
stories today until the
dwindling stars beg her
off to sleep where she
will dream the Word
made flesh. tomorrow,
she will begin the day
whispering the names
of friends who will met
her in school with bright
red flowers.

SHORTY

I poured water into a
bottle from the leaking
pump in the middle of

the block. it was midnight
when the street began to
let go of the bodies that

wished to fall quietly into
sleep and kids were told be
afraid of the dark. three of

us aged ten were out on the
stoop with Shorty whose mother
just lost a skimpy apartment

a week earlier and with a troubled
soul was bouncing around the
neighborhood staying with friends.

she was then in Lela's apartment
talking about unemployment, the
church, the rosary and hell. Shorty

was on the stoop taking a drink of
water to wash down some gloom.
the breeze blowing must have come

that night from the desert crossed
by the family in Apartment 5C
adjusting to life on Home Street.

I was sitting once again on that stoop
with friends thinking about Shorty who
joined the Marines to escape the block

but shortly after was escorted from life
in a Vietnamese field. his good name is
on the memorial in the nation's capital

where some of us god knows go once a
year to visit. the monolingual president
who especially hates Spanish will never

say his real name right and campaigning
for his Wall of shame will keep him busy
with the bullshit doctrine of manifest destiny

stretching his mouth from sea-to-sea
while he shouts giddy up on millions of
hammered down people from way down

South and the Caribbean Sea.

JAILED

there's plenty of need for us
in the fields and pitiful work

places but a xenophobic Congress
would have everyone believe we

are plain old criminals that must
leave. in these strange times

it is a crime to dream of a better
life in Black and Brown, a time

when mothers with gang targeted
kids are denied sanctuary, kept

separate from their young and
criminally charged for crossing

the border without permission.
even people who know how to

kneel believe escaping danger
is intolerable wrongdoing that

their reading of the Holy Book
cannot change. they would be

surprised to learn the lives mowed
down at the border, on the streets,

by errant politicians, and hidden
for-profit jails are today's sign of

the man hanging from a tree. it is
a crime to talk about the kid's faces

with tears, huddled together in cages,
pleading for their families and begging

to be set free—the whips keep cracking!
what will they do, next?

WE, THE PEOPLE

listening to the day begin
to wake, seeing the gentle
light stretching across the
sky, I think about ancestors
who traveled across the sea,
walked over the phony border,
served in American foreign
wars, settled in big cities to
clean offices, toilets, windows,
and upper-class things with a
whole lotta of other brown people
like me. they made a living with
bloody sweat, wrecked backs,
and injured hearts that were
daily schooled by an ungrateful
state's hate.   listening to the
morning songs, the rustling of
pale green trees, I recall these
people of the border who walked

were filled with dreams, scars still rattling old slavers chains and the will to make immigrant America great!

THE NEIGHBORS

the apartment next to me
had people in it though I

never saw them open their
door wide. I once saw a sofa

leaning against a wall with
fresh store tags that appeared

destined along with a Quaker
style chair beside it for the space.

I can't tell you when these two
things were taken inside but

everything was gone from the
hallway by midnight. the gossip

in the building talked by several
Puerto Rican girls hoarding it like

delicious flan from the cuchifrito
restaurant said the people in 5B

were from the only country in
Africa that spoke Spanish better

than us. we don't have fences
in tenements for neighbors and we

can be swept around the moon for
years with foolish questions for the

people next door, so I knocked one
day but there was no answer and

the next morning on the long walk
to public school, I imagined the

invisible family in the apartment
were as close to happiness as the

rest of the block.

THE PARTY

after a little more than an
hour the talking wore out,
laughter dulled the noise
from the world pounding
in our heads, the candles
in the fireplace veiled light
without end, sweet sounds
of Spanish warmed every
space, plates of communion
held flat-corn like Salvadoran
bread, music flew around the
room like a bird in a cage just
let out, we heard two women
sacredly speak, formed a big
circle to braid them a prayer,
allowed all the festal spirits to
rise beneath our skin, and danced
into night for the sake of God's
name. at the end of the party,

with grace settled in, we returned
to creation with fewer old scars
and promises to offer others more
love.

THE LAST DAYS

the death of kindness can now be
seen loitering the border to fill little
girls who saw their brothers die
with perfect fear. every day they
end the long walk to come looking
for the place that made many others
safe, their staggering lives purchased
with a price, faces like a rugged map
detailing harsh flight, dressed with
the shadows of night, knocking at the
locked door of another country drenched
with Spanish speaking blood, and the
sweet word liberty tripping from parched
white tongues. just looking at the faces
of the cruel greying men that happily punish
these poor and never sorrow about the lives
swinging on bending trees until death takes
them makes you cry. without end, mountains,
rivers, trees, seas and the simple rocks on ancient

lanes shout today America where are your shining cities set upon the hills? America where has your beauty gone? America what have you betrayed?

THE HOSPITAL

after many years there are
stories to tell of the sky blue
thunderbird parked on Mapes
Avenue, the old rocking chair
in front of a television with a
hanger antenna in the living
room, the parakeet won at a
roulette table for a dime, the
nights pressed into the sofa
for prayer, the simple things
in your dreams and the sweat
running down backs at Orchard
Beach on the hot long days of
Summer. there are stories about
the hospital bed with a bandaged
head, nurses gossiping of your
Lucifer boyfriend, life without
peace, friends without papers,
bony kids with Spanglish speech,
and your firm determination to
live. there are stories to tell of

the water poured on your lips,
the opiates to ease your heaping
pain and now heaven swinging
low for your last breath. there
are stories about swollen hearts,
candles set aflame in the dark,
and a heavy day that will always
hear us say woman your love in
this world remains.

TAKING IN THE LIGHT

you are worth more than the
riches adorning the stony hearts

of those who foul the sweet
smell of things and steal the

bread of the poor struggling
with life to make beauty from

little things. it cannot be said
by any of the world's callous

men your labor is a worthless
thing, your back made for their

lashes, your children destined
for early graves and the daily

experience of being stomped
beneath white feet.   you are

worth more than heaven far
from earth, the feeble efforts

of the prince of peace, liberty
that sees no wrong, philosophy

denying you equality, and the
felon hands of politicians that

convict you for having no more
than darker skin. from the ground

on which you stand with your
heart that explores the streets,

sanctuaries, workplaces and the
capital steps recall when feeling

weak you live between injury and
courage with God on earth.

THE BORDER

come to the border to see
how the future is written

in tears, to look upon the
wounded flesh in sealed

cages, mothers dragged
from children, fathers in

cells hanging themselves
with grief. come listen at

the border to the sociable
talk of uniformed men who

whack away at the migrant
poor, listen to them laugh at

the asylum seekers slipped
into anguish, watch them

pace the day with the barbed
wired words of the rich man

suffered up by a misguided
electorate for president. take

your first steps into the land
familiar to the bastard Christ

from Palestine, etch the faces
without names on your heart,

take them to bed tonight, wake
with them at the morning light,

learn their Spanish names, let
your eyes weep at the sight of the

dismal tax paid jails, get hold of
ethical sanity and rescue from

State evil the condemned.

IN MY SKIN

they cannot hear the screams of
frightened children in I.C.E. cages,

adrift in the madness of a world
wickedly declared by an immigrant

first lady in wardrobe that might as
well have been nasty white sheets

say, "I don't really care, do you?" they
cannot see with their blood shot eyes

the thousands of Christs in helpless
flight, the weary daughters in search of

hope, the skinny sons nearly snatched
from life, the terrifying walks in the

dead of night, the sad look in baptized
strangers' eyes and how much it hurts

to be homeless, spat upon, split apart
and jailed. they find a million reasons

to let Spanish speakers perish, to make
brown skin a crime, to inspire mighty

white hands to press us into earth and
to tell the world hate is the divine plan.

they will never strip us with white hell
of paradise in our love, prevent stones

from crying out our names, drown us
in our tears or keep us from scattering

truth with pained words on the White
House wall of lies. these fools who think

they are righteously leading simply fail
to see our sanctuary is this beautiful brown

skin created by a radically kind and ever
welcoming Black God.

KIN

I returned from a foreign
shore to walk these city

streets more clumsily than
ever, confessing the world

is too enormous to think,
pausing on the corners to

take in the latest news of
coldhearted times, hearing

words from people who find
they survive coughing up hope.

I tremble at the sight of the
reminders of empire waving

us to move along, the politics
of brutes more steadily mounting

our terrified hearts, the leaders
spreading the plague burying what

is left of virtue with their tongues
and our children confessing a lesser

god has made us. the dark days
have a way about them that

untangles light to let us see
who hangs on trees with final

breaths begging for justice to
come out of its hiding place

to take on the foul-mouthed thug
behaving like Hitler's English

speaking kin.

BETRAYAL

the sun has drained
the coolness from last
nights sidewalk. today
we see more clearly the
things untrue that just
yesterday poured into
us. the money men in
the capital pass currency
between them and call it
public works, the blessed
children come on the street
to play, the elderly sit on
their beach chairs holding
umbrellas and we wait to
end the news filled day in
another round of screams. by
midday the flag will wither
a little more to the sound of
washed-up speeches selling
empty days and more lusty
hate to come. who will pull

the veil from our eyes and smite
the absurd acts of those elected
to betray? who will even share
the faintest whisper to have the
country back? who will speak
for kindness and talk still of
the American social creed?
speak, please, speak!

BREAD

an elderly woman with a
red Minnie Mouse tee-shirt
is rummaging her house in a
box. she wheeled it to the
parking lot in a wire carriage
placed it on the hood of a
black jaguar to look inside it
for things with old stories.
sometimes, she sits on the
pavement in front of shops,
picks flowers along her walks
from public lots, and adds to
a page with a favorite pen a
line about friends never near
for dinner, the apartment with
high costs and old age in a
homeless way. tonight, when
she is full of sleep I will visit
with her beneath the highway
to break bread.

THE CANDLE

when you light a candle
in the name of your sister
who has gone in search of
refuge with her two young
boys she rescued from gangs,
notice the chair in the corner
of the room, her tattered bible
beside it, the smiling pictures
on the wall hanging by the head
of big nails and the things that
are enough to keep her home.
while the candle burns in honor
of her, comfort your old mother
who misses her dearest friend,
pray for the frightened boys making
the long walk and what remains
of laughter in her four tiny rooms.
when you sit beside the flame, notice
the light shining in darkness, how the
shadows lean and the silence pushes
its way to hope. when the candle

burns away, light another with its flame, let the new one also be on speaking terms, never talk to it of wicked things, let it burn away the aches, and plead with it until the mutes up north contest their cruel days and the dust settles.

THE LINE

the border is a line you cannot
see, the meeting place of north

and south, a stop once safe for
kids. the border is a bruising

fence with cracked uniformed
hearts, a wailing wall rejecting

longing souls, the clown's spot
that swallows dreams whole. the

border is a shut door to another
home, the place hunger lurks, nights

filled with cold and bloody feet that
halt before a North supplied with lots

of hate. the border is the night
in sadness ringing, the earth beneath

the migrants' feet declaring without
permission come, exhausted friends

on the other side with kind faces that
wait to brush them clean of dust, and in

the houses of prayer a few prophets
who dare a speech. the border is where

you see wounded flesh, mothers dragged
from howling kids, cages polished up

for the innocent, fathers given a noose
for their grief, jailers laughing as they

work and taxes sinfully spent. the
border is where migrants recite in

Spanish: Lord give the blind sight, help
the lame walk, the deaf hear and deliver

us from evil.

NO ROAD

every speech adds nothing
to change the silence, to tell
us who is stealing the light, or
what keeps love from warming
us. no one any longer explains
the fast running of the lapping
river, the reasons why we cross,
the faint hope wading across with
us, or the hate exuding from the
Lilly White House with polished
floors, paintings, memories and
paradise thrown to the floor. no
one spells out the disappearance
of tenderness, our lonely desert
deaths, days looking like an old
bus full of dirt, and why so many
in America live without tongues.
only the wind knows our wet eyes,
dares to say this way home, pushes
when we want to turn back, embraces
us without knowing our names or

checking the color of our skin. maybe
one day they'll allow us to mumble
at their fence while standing on the
corpses of our baptized kids God
forgive their inhumanity but make
them change.

THE MARCH

in the passing year, a last testament
of a Black professor was written about

a life resolved to say things unheard
of the One who deployed mystery in

the world. in a different country south
of the equator, where ancient tides slip

soberly to shore, and birds still love
to lift their voices in the wind, another

final testament begins in the mind of
a priest who untangled the poor from

dogmatic ways of thought. they told
us to pay reverence to divinity battered

in Black and Brown skin, denouncing
the sin of the unkind, questioning the

odd gods to whom the rich knelt and
taking the silence on the cross, the brutal

death of slaves, into our souls' depths
to hear we are free. how blind we have

become to the One who came among
us poor, who preached with open arms,

and found so many reasons to weep! I
wonder will we ever hurry to embrace?

will we ever confess the holy book's
evidence of love creeping closer to the

wretched of the earth? the great cloud
of witnesses say one day we shall hear

the cries of the oppressed and know,
completely!

GRACE

I should lean into your ear
to say the mountains will one
day be pocket size, the young
will gather by the open gate to
begin treading down the hilly
lanes, the greedy old men and
the crooked dreams left making
speeches on the church steps. I
should whisper the length of the
year stories about children who
lived beside the tracks of the third
Avenue subway, who faced unkind
struggle yet endured, prayed to a
God in creaturely flesh, looked for
the light of candles in darkening
days of hate and made their way
to the creek known as the place
for washing feet. I should tell you
of aging for years in their skin, smiling
at the shadows that still break across
their faces, feeling them come to me

in shouts from the border loud enough
to nearly break the pretty rose windows
in high-minded churches so far from
God. imagine, a misfit president no longer
on TV, a White House image that can't
pimple your skin, and the thought of the
Helper from ages past living in the shadow
of an empire made by the blood of Indians,
Africans and all the poor. I should tell you
this grace makes my eyes heavily wet with
laughter!

THE TODDLERS

today the protest signs are
lifted high for toddlers in

court with third hand shoes
climbing on a desk, while

the judges stare directly into
their guiltless little eyes asking

with odd sounding words why
did you come. they cannot talk

about the necks cut in their
villages, the bodies charred

by lunacy, the gangsters on
the streets who made them

flee by foot for the long and
tired march toward sanctuary

in a Northern world they also
fail to understand. today, the

protest signs remind us these
little ones know nothing of the

border they have crossed, the
flawed hearts that ordered them

into cages, the guards for hire who
laugh when they cry, the first lady

who doesn't really care, and Christian
citizens giving thanks not to be brown

like them. these undocumented boys
and girls barely able to speak in full

Spanish sentences, taken from the
hands of mothers who were thrown

like criminals in prison are the blessed
poor a lying government wants to send

away in the name of white justice.
today we carry our saddest cares to

heaven and vigorously march to expose
the evil deeds of bitter politicians who

feed on innocent blood.

HEAVENLY

the name of the street where
sorrow lurks in ambush is

recalled clearer than a first
love, the cool winds of the

Fall filled with the scent of
the ocean, the endless feeling

of finding a way, the ancient
gods tenderly caressing the

aches, trees in the little park
given Spanish names and light

older than the earth quietly moving
around us. how many have left

their years on that old street,
watched shadows roam sidewalks,

heard open windows cry, carried
the playful voices of children to

work and adorned themselves with
love? eternity may very well be

the warm sunrise, the angels on the
rooftops weeping, the lantern moon

seen from the beginning stubbornly
lighting the night, the forgotten joys

of home, the open books that have
never understood a thing and the simple

truths still delighting us with daily
odd things. perhaps, it's not too

late to leave our load on the roadside
to make ready for less back-breaking

days.

HELL

when children reached the
border the president's men
trembled with fear. they turned
words in their heads trying to
explain the weak terrifying
them, making up stories of
mothers with kids reduced
to more suffering, creeping
around the capital with scaled
eyes and inspiring a nation to
hate the asylum seekers tangled
up in chains. little do they care
of the gold handcuffs crushing
life from their veins, the holy
words that condemn their sins,
the Crucified God hidden in
brown skin, and the Angels
with barbed wire hats grieving
with the outcasts sliding their
hands across an American made
fence. before you set foot on the

border be prepared to hear the howling of the descendants of slaves, the poor who mourn and children who weep. notice they cannot be consigned to loathsome sinking in the sand or swept far from the triumphs of love. yes, the old men afraid of the meek will one day be belly down in their tombs, tied tightly to the earth and never see the heaven their actions detest.

THE WATER

from the waves endlessly
making their way to shore

out of a mystic ocean, the
lovers throwing themselves

on the sand, the old woman
at the water's edge a little child

again, the feathered guests on
the seashore cautiously looking,

pacing, searching, the scent of
summer is in the air with the

language of the restless sea.
from the wind blowing the

songs of a radio, the sound of a
distant barking dog, the plain day

with delicious secrets to whisper,
you with wondrous thoughts lay

waiting patiently for truth to
kindle visibly like the half-moon

that is beginning to hang in the
heavens. we can agree this time

is worth saving like the memory of
the spirit that once moved upon

the face of the waters.

THEY CROSS THE BORDER

they travel with homes stuffed
into small bags, sleep in fields,

on hard dirt floors, bus station
benches, on tractor trains, beside

the rivers that have for centuries
rounded hills, and beneath distant

stars hanging like lanterns in an
ancient sky. along the underground

railroad on the long walk toward the
border, light on the walls of Spanish

speaking shacks open their eyes to
the simple frailty of life, the voices

fled in grief, the choking feeling in
the company of other women and

children walking away from endless
poverty and violence that they will

be changed and their children by the
year's end no longer recognized. in

lucid moments they stare at evening
stars blinking stories of hate waiting

to include them at the border, offering
quiet prayers to God who hides in the

black patches between dots of celestial
light forgetting to comfort them. they

have strolled Sunday shoes old in less
than forty days, El Norte drawing near

with each long step, children insisting
with occasional tears they can keep the

pace, giving illness in their long days
new names, trying to reach America

scrubbed fresh with dreams, hoping when
they come up against the southern wall

they are not named poison or unwanted
filth by the Lilly white people who live

behind locked doors on stolen land.

LIES

children from another
shore bitterly mocked for

your poverty and dark skin,
English terror whispered in

your innocent ears, governors
without fear of God tossing

you in cages, villages you fled
pityingly existing in knee bending

fear, crumbs of old bread dangling
on the edges of your lips, drawing

inside yourself more by the hour,
experiencing mothers hopes come

to nothing in El Norte that trembles
when you speak Spanish, the ancients

of this land have said their savage
delusions cannot out last your endless

nerve to not turn back your tiny feet.
children who weep your tears making

the oceans deep, tonight just before you
sleep the wistful sages will again sing

God in you cannot be turned away for
the sake of border threat lies!

NIGHT

one night in a dream that
came in the shadows of a
tiny apartment, the thick
talk of America that walled
me into a black and white
world came apart, I saw
the stunning people of the
barrio never welcomed in
their country with beautiful
brown faces, dark hands, and
lively Spanish tongues. in our
rented rooms, kids Spanglish
voices came through the walls
like the call of olden drums,
mothers prayed to Saints, black
Gods, and strangely named spirits,
and the windows of the city
blew open. on that night, I saw
Lefty who went to heaven from
the Bronx, wearing thrift store
jeans, a wrinkled Delancey Street

shirt, with wet eyes waving from the far distance until out of sight. I heard time crying for us like a sinner in the confession box, and brown faces in a sea of black and white bodies wept.

HARMONY

the day in waking is quiet
like monks in silent prayer,
nature in her process speaks
of adoration, the divine finds
a way to sparkle inside things
and the melancholy hearts turn
suddenly to have a look. protests
are exempt now, no one is asked
to speak, and we are all tempted
by the tranquility of morning to
admit our destination without a
wasted tear will be reached.

WORD

where does the tenderness
holding children's hands in

the long walk come from?
how does love in these

mother's hearts who were
beaten, threatened, raped

and mocked grow despite
the crushing hate? why do

they give thanks lighting
candles in Cathedrals, saying

prayer in detention cells and
remembering the savior in a

world of forgotten poor? how
do they know when the maker

of all things finally descends
pointing a finger at the insane

world to make things change?
where do the words they write

on cardboard and scraps of paper
cursing unrepentant politicians

with flawless hate come from?
only they can tell us to make this

battered world of clay whole!

WICKEDNESS

the men of currency who lick
their lips, dance deep into night

draped in vile sheets and delight
in the ghastly passing of Brown

bodies swinging in detention cells
will never be forgiven their sins.

the Creator who looks upon the
earth, who died tormented by the

wicked, powerful and criminally
rich, hidden in the suffering, the

maimed, and those crushed into
hard graves never swore to save

cruel old men like these. the world,
as it must be, is revealed by the

bleeding hearts of children who
wipe away each other's tears, the

broken who hold on to love and
the shithole people who despite

the legions of hate walked North
with the prayers of priests and

village shamans offering decrees
of life. the men of currency who

hinder light in their minds, are in
love with lies and love sounding

off about their power, will see
sweetness, warmth, and peace

beyond their reach on their day
of final rest when they will beg

God for mercy, justice and love!

BUS STOP

at the bus stop two people
argue about how much
dark is covering the island
after the hurricane named
for the Mother of God hit
land, they breathe deeply to
shake their heads about the
nearly five thousand dead
never mentioned on white
news, their names not once
treated in the English papers
to kind print and the radios
that are full of chatter about
his fucken Wall. they are tired
of night coming slowly, need
no papers to live poor in city
tenements and never say a
word of praise for the lofty
ignorance spreading across
America like a plague.

THE ISLAND

I wrote my name on a wall
in old San Juan 40 years
ago thinking I lived in my
mother's paradise where
there was no need to look
back or ahead. I saw kindness
stumble out of the sea, the
things grandmothers knew by
touch, the places that talked
to me of everything my people
had once been, the old churches
where priests spoke to me like
God just dropped me on the soft
rain forest hills and the brown earth
beaten by rain that dissolved aches
in Boricua hearts. the island was
never silent, fierce winds have not
blown out the lighted candles buried
by mother in my soul and I hear her
drums preparing for a day that kicks
up sand across the ocean to the White
House steps!

THE STROLL

here we are so many years later
the warming sun no different, the
sidewalks yet quietly catching what
is sent of light, inhabiting memories
that creep out from behind the heart's
curtains, recollecting the blues guitar
player with brown hands tossing his
soul at us, lovers everywhere listening
and scaling their sadness with devouring
kisses, the patter of children's feet pulling
us toward very gentle smiles, not wanting
to let this moment, depart. here we are
after scaling walls by the year, weeping
about the slave ships that came into this
port, catching sight of the well-off walking
into a church built on grandmothers soiled
earth, wondering about the day when the
whirlwind will change direction to take
us in. here we are strolling in these old
shoes wanting to tell our children who will
grow into them, everything.

CAGE

the little boy sits in his
American cage staring
day after day at the odd
food placed in front of
him, waiting for word
about his mother, and
drinking tears that accuse
heaven of not breaking his
chains. the guards are paid
to keep the child's witness
from the world, to tell the
little brown face there is no
place to go, the American air
breathed is not for him and
mommy will not be coming
to sing him to sleep. the little
boy by light was given a name,
carved on trees far away, dreaded
by odious know nothing lips kept
fed by a loveless government and
ignorant of what makes each one

of us human beings. the little boy
wipes his wet dark eyes, clutches
the silver wires of his cage, looks
everywhere for a hint of liberty and
with belief born in a tiny village
church waits for his mother and a
new life to spread open before him.
when the lights in the huge room
go out, he quietly sobs in the dark,
expecting an oracular voice to burst
into the prison with good news for
his journey.

EARTHLY DUST

they were beaten into
the long walk, their eyes

wide with hunger looking
upon the border, with nothing

criminal about them, moving
among the weary with perfect

courage to take flight, telling
others along the way in a clear

voice their truth, watching the
mystic moon on summer nights,

composing songs in their hearts
about the lot god has cast upon

innocent lives and eager for a
new place to call home. on the

other side of the line, in the far
country with hateful odd picketers,

these citizens filled with ignorant
gossip wait with fresh crowns of

thorn. then, shouted prayers stir
the jail cells about life not freely

given by an English only God to
those who mourn the contempt

exiling them to death. at night,
their voices fall on perfect silence

and hope in these fucken cages
buds like flowers leaning toward

a warming light.

POSTERITY

he wishes perfect flowers
tossed before his feet on
walks, approval showering
his head from heaven, the
half thoughts tossed in public
not ever heard obtuse, and his
interest in making a nation
great not confused with hate
for non-white people dying
by the print left by his brand
name pen on tax paid paper.
his worldly tasks grab support
from politicians of witchery
charm, while children on the
southern border are consigned
to cages with broken hearts.
this man who ruins earth with
decisions invented beneath a
draped white sheet, who turns
vulnerable flesh into bread to
feed his puffy flushed cheeks,

eager to step on others, thrilled to condemn, stirring the thirst for blood in people content to string up their darker fellow citizens by the neck, wants posterity to keep silent about his crimes against humanity, imbecility and hate. America will dream again tomorrow for herself and without cowering will tell stories about the man desiring admiration for shaking hands with the devil!

ALPHABET CITY

I walked by the supermarket on
avenue C smiling at the faces in
the Ukrainian restaurants noticing
food on carts in front of bodegas
wondering why so many people
on the Lower East Side still go
hungry. they still recite Hebrew
prayers from the storefront temples
on the ground floor of the cheapest
buildings, kids play on sidewalks in
front of them and jump around yelling
imaginative Spanish, Catholic mothers
hang on the stoops talking about a trip
to Delancey Street to buy church clothes
priced lower than Macys and I ask
Lord why with two jobs the city eats
them up. I stroll beneath a bright urban
sky stubbornly looking for a sacramental
sign, becoming more speechless inside
about a world that does not believe limping
people are worth mentioning and press

my palms together on Houston Street by
the corner light to say God dismiss the
useless churches, tell the choirs not to
sing and show up to sit on the stoops with
your stone swallowing people trying to
find better days.

RAIN

the trees drink the persistent
rain, today. the gentle drops
land on the sidewalk making
memories bubble to the surface
about how you love mornings
that start with wet neon signs
chilled by waterflow from the
sky. yesterday will be washed
clean by the drops pooling on
the city streets, the wet kisses
streaming down our faces, the
distant rivers that fall today from
above to lift us closer to the
secrets of certainty and tease us
with the groaning clouds toward
moments of perfect wholeness.
we are handed the rain to drink,
the sweet water for living and
now this love in due season put
forth from heaven.

LAST BREATH

I know the place with stained
wood confessionals, the kneeling

rail visited by the obedient for
relief, the simple altar many say

weeps with pity, the image of
Mary in the sanctuary's distant

corner an Angel said would for
nine months carry freedom in

her womb, the questioning pews
where mothers sit dimly sensing

time with peace, this last place
on earth where God never leaves

us alone. many years ago, I found
its door open, saw candles playing

in darkness, the sound of whispers
tossing Spanish voices out to the

stained street and entered to sit
next to an old man who insisted

holding my hand that Angel's feet
never make a sound. I lost track

of time sitting on a bench at the
rear of the sanctuary close to the

exit, waited for the secret of life
to be disclosed and even prayed

for the dust of the earth to stand
up when I called out names. that

place became a divine presence
for me, a bell to accompany what

is glad in the aching flesh of the
block rescued by the last breath

on the cross at Golgotha.

DREAMER

he cleans the subway station
through the early morning hours

of the city, thousands of dreams
call to him on his shift, his hands

ache from pushing a broom for hours
and he dislikes the old tenement

in the Bronx that strips its renters
of life. he dreams of opening a bodega

on the corner of Westchester Avenue,
a store people can forget nightmarish

places and young Puerto Rican mothers
buying diapers on credit can visit often

to discover brown visions of a future
patched with sweet grass. on the corner,

la bodega would never run out of things,
Muslims would have a spot by the Café

Bustelo to fulfill mandatory prayers, his
mother's Rosary would hang on a wall

above the votive candles with images of
Christ next to the cold beer, fresh Valencia

Bakery bread would rest in baskets laughing
through the morning and the high school

gangsters baptized in the Catholic church
around the corner would enter to stash ideas

about another way of life. by the end of one
sweaty work shift, he came up with a name

for la bodega, Angel's Place—and smiled!

REHAB

when you get to the hospital on
first avenue, where Ana gave

birth, the one that treats junkie
old men who no longer speak,

where Francis has worked for the
past fifteen years, tell the counselor

why you love to sit in the church
with stained glass windows after

shooting dope on the roof. in the
waiting room, brush off the Monday

morning sadness, take a good look
at the fading stars above your fresh

out of Jesus head and try not to empty
the rehab room with all the lies you

tell about life. remember over the
next twenty-one days, when your

feet touch the cold floor and the addict
inside of you begins to peel away like

a broken toe nail, God will find a way
to hold your hand like a lover saying

you have never been more alive. we
will wait for you on the corner where

the Mexican women selling tamales to
Boricuas from plump hands talk to

customers about the land of milk and
honey that overlooks no one.

FAILE STREET

when they asked me what it
was like to walk nights in the
shadow of old street lights, I
said it was like a subway ride
on a dark morning with a cold
chill, alone. when they wondered
how I was able to stand for hours
on the corner begging for change,
walk the city alleys searching
rubbish bins for nourishment,
I said, homeless.   when they
pointed to the scar on my right
wrist demanding to know how
it got there, I paused like a
lazy postman then answered,
a knife. when they questioned
the violence in the place of my
birth, the lives that marched off
like numbers with the saints, I
said we have dreams bigger than
bible tales. when they were just

about to speak again, I whispered
in this slum where flowers turn
into cement blocks, we eat the
apples given in the Garden of
Eden on Faile Street.

ESTHER

we walked the streets last
night talking until we got

to Tito's café, imagining
on the long tread between

two city bridges the way
bright Spanish names are

detested and how the current
government takes macabre steps

to keep brown skinned women
and children from bearing witness

to American crimes in their world.
we sat sometimes for long periods

in silence to keep from crying,
near broken hearts swearing in two

languages at the bullshit of these
third millennium days, displaying

crazed eyes around the table, taking
turns shouting expletives at a God

unresponsive to prayer and the sorrows
puncturing our souls. we talked into

the early morning hours, at one point
wondering whether or not a blurred

face of Jesus would appear in the
mirror behind the bar receiving the

faces of people sitting on stools who
sweetened their lips with drink. time

came that Esther reached into her bag
to pull out a folded map that was still

weeping from her long walk across
three countries, then with lowered

eyes and a shaking head, she sighed
hate will outlive us, here—mierda!

KNEEL

I have grown old recalling days
kneeling with my brother on rice

in the apartment hallway, noisy
neighbors shouting on the steps,

the uptown bus' fumes floating
through the crack on the old front

door with the Star of David still
pasted above the doorframe that

even today keeps me curious.
I remember the very first hymn

sung in the Catholic church up
the street, where a young priest

I learned baptized me with the
fresh certainty of knowing the

future of the Bronx, the place
widows splintered by the slum

said prayers, and Puerto Rican
families sat silently waiting for

their larger than the Hoe Avenue
church Savior to show. I survived

forsaken times, traveled about the
edges of cities and Latin villages

with more than a handful of hurt
beliefs, looked at the earth promised

to the meek, and tried to evade the
idea that lifting my arms to heaven

is pointless. I recall eating some of the
grains of rice to make punished knees

hurt less, asking clouds to cry for me
and light to rush into the South Bronx

shadows mercilessly disabling
the poor.

THE NIGHTMARE

I had a dream last night about
wandering the border, starry

heavens blackening with each
step, kids on the Mexican side

of the fence setting tires on fire,
mothers on their knees weeping,

old men with swollen feet turning
into dust, Angels with cut wings

singing to infants unaware of their
escape and stray dogs licking young

hands wrinkled from hard work.
I saw an altar just beneath a watch

tower, an unbroken loaf of bread
resting on a plate, a feeble flame

on a candle next to an opened bible
with torn pages, a skeleton hand

searching through it and brown
people gathered around it turning

into hard clay. I looked at heaven
to argue with the Highest against

faith turning into a grave, darkness
offered instead of aid, and innocent

lives condemned by heartless fiends
to an agonizing death.

DEPORTED

you remember the day
Ana got up early to get

her two American made
kids to school, stumbling

with her dreams down a
flight of old steps in the

tenement, with that look
in her eyes saying a voice

from the sky was speaking
Spanish to her, and how

her lips trembled when the
idea of a work place raid

by I.C.E. was mentioned in
front of the building. do you

still hear the church bells that
rang loudly that morning, the

sound rippling the space on
the sidewalk without giving

us a hint of the promises of
Christ perverted by churchy

words, and Ana waving until
later to us who sat quietly on

the stoop. do you recall the
protests the night she never

made it home from work,
her children weeping in Tia

Lela's arms, and the widows
in black dress decrying the

migra who rounded Ana up
at work are not of God! tell

me what happened to those
kids and the mother deported

to her country so full of Christian
martyrs?

APARTMENT

I dwell in the tenement
with people shouting out

names imported like dark
roast coffee to the city, the

building where maternal
hands in brown shades hold

infants to pray and children
make up Spanish games that

rush to other apartments like
novel songs. I am but a fifth

floor resident waiting for the
old familiar faces to come up

the steps, for the purely drained
to open a door and step into the

hallway to give that certain look
bound for somewhere. I dwell

near the park with clustering leaves,
in the land thriving with ill-informed

tongues, overlooked by the savior's
pain, with icy ground melting beneath

the feet on people demanding life and
bread.

LABOR DAY

on this gray September day
when workers find reason to
sleep, the buses run slowly,
the trains glide into stations
with few who care, laborers
who roam the quiet streets
question yet another shifty
tweet about the best of times
they call misery. noiseless
Labor Day hours disclose the
hardened faces that carry
stalled prayers in old pockets
while the man who promised
better days only gets a little
richer. the sweaty people with
weary limbs who love this
day for talk, touched for weeks
by darkness, lament the men
in leadership who cater labor's
dreams with crap.

THE FORGOTTEN

I have looked for them
in the dark back alleys,

the sleepless nights, the
littered streets, trampled

church steps, the candles
that flicker on the Saintly

altars, furniture in tenement
apartments freshly dressed

with plastic covers and the
names gathering dust on

mailboxes in the hall and
big cemetery. I looked for

them in needles going into
young veins, Joseph going to

prison, Julia dropping out
of seventh grade, Carmen

crumbling slowly beside her
bottle, Hector with an arm

displaced by a bullet to a city
owned incinerator. I searched

the shadows on the corners,
the river where five-year-old

Sonia drowned, the old buses,
steel wheeled trains, the stars

and invisible wind and cried
when Angels never come. now,

I know they have forgotten us
and cannot see or feel people

who live in slums.

PUBLIC SCHOOL

today I wonder how different
public school would be in the

barrio, where Spanish words
sink deeply into fleshy hearts

carried in thin bodies by kids
tarnished by teachers who can

only call them thugs. I began
to cry for them in the just out

sun, sent by the unthinking
God too satisfied to make a

little time to see how separate
and unequal education beats

up on knowledge starved and
doggedly policed kids without

white skin. in my broken up
soul, where I still carry around

a crowded single-room, where
single mothers yet gather at

night praying to fall into the
hands of the Lord, I sob about

so much official wrong doing.
with trembling hands opening

the ripped pages of the Holy
book, I hang sacred hope in public

spaces for others to see. today,
I wonder how different my beloved

slum would be if the wind carried
the screams that ask: what's God

got to do with us?

THE CLOCKS

we live in a world full of
borders made by words

that have no need at all
for them, sweetly holding

hands in the dark while
the builders of big impious

walls spit in the wind, and
the beaten down cry in all

the languages of the earth. we
live like stuttering facts in

the shadows, selling food
off carts from coast to coast

barrios, creating no less a world
with Spanish tongues, staying

a few steps ahead of hate and
in our ways searching on corners,

streets, schools, work and even
the apathetic church for light.

we live in a world that pleas
not to be counted other, always

probing the hearts of the free,
sentenced to prison, awaiting

with fragile souls for someone
to look for us and stand in line

beside us.

THE FIRE

standing on the corner
strangely still at the edge

of the city, Tito in his
apartment with windows

rattling Morse code when
buses roll pass, the shouts

against the darkness startling
pigeons confused about the

noise passing for wisdom,
while elderly men play cards

in front of the dream selling
bodega and whisper to each

other things about their world
in change. life is short! on the

wall behind us the painted names
of those who ended here, local

priests still bless it with tongue
biting prayers, and at night we

show up again to place candles
that question Paul's sacred letter

saying death is the highest form of
freedom. soon, we will allow the

swarm of words festering in these
bellies to scream like demented

swallows to lay to waste the chains
that keep us bitter, suffering, and

barely alive! we keep looking up
at the sky expecting graffiti to

stretch across it until hope for
us comes into full view and a

new day begins with all the
preachers said it is cracked up

to be. but, tonight, we think
paradise was long ago lost in

flames!

THE JUDGE

I go up the street to the
newspaper stand in the

faint morning light and
slowly read dark print

words reporting the spin
the president's men make

to excuse the hands that
galloped on the body of a

female classmate. they sit
with tongues like butcher

sharpened knives denying
the unimpeachable pain of

a woman the Supreme Court
nominee corralled one day

to touch with a nightmare
that never leaves. women in

heaven even now relive the
damage, feel the miles of

scars, and shout thy will be
done on earth. I go up the street

carrying the autumn in my
arms, noticing the flag withering

on a pole flying in front of City
Hall, hearing Dr. Ford call my

name and feeling her cross on
my back I realize as she leans

forward a precious human
being speaks.

SOPHIA

now, the candles shed
light to help us step into

a watery day that tossed
us like a pebble in a lost

hand. the helpless many
across the nation know first

hand that facts were never
worthy to the politicians

with high seats who gave each
other flowers to congratulate

pure deceit. the candles greet
us now with cool sympathy,

their gentle flare in growing
darkness urging us to strive

beyond the brute hour, and
into the timelessness of the

day hope will make good!
today, the candles brightly

dance in shadows, on the saintly
altars kept in the homes of

the poor, in the big empty
churches worshipping God

as a privileged White man,
to mock the twisted faces

thinned bit by bit of truth.

HERESY

each year offers a new
season to doubt most

everything I ever heard
in churches that are now

nameless. the world with
extravagant style has a

way of tempting me with
the most exquisite forms

of misunderstanding that
simply cannot be thrown

away. the barbaric silence
of the good people, the love

choked by the crying poor
standing on cracked earth,

the abundance paraded in
front of ravening children,

the paradise that is not ever
breathed, the undocumented

staggering at the end of them
long walks, the nonstop rancid

prayers and the grisly thought
that truth is reality in tooth and

claw. there are enough reasons
to be smothered with questions,

to believe heaven is deaf and
God no more than a self-satisfied

mute. each year I find myself on
beloved slum corners speaking with

others in the flesh wishing a few
choice words of heresy might at last

unmask the Highest grandmothers
said is between things.

LORD

Lord, my tears think of
you on the paths where
you are voiceless, in the
fields that make us bleed,
the sweatshops that feed on
injured flesh, and places that
leave us voiceless. Lord, do
you know those shouting are
older than your moon, purer
than your brightest dreams,
and more beautiful than your
secret garden. sweet Lord, that
last drop of blood on ancient
wood has left you silent and
vaguely recollecting we live
in your ingenious hell. Lord, take
a long look in our direction, push
aside the darkness and name us
with a simple touch.

SACRILEGE

the suffering on Simpson Street
that never matters downtown and

for people who believe themselves
protected by prayer points by the

minute to an imperfect God who
was present from the beginning.

the rise and fall of the poor and
those inhumanly named spic lead

us with a South Bronx chattering
wind to such certainty. I was told

in pretty churches to hold on to the
substance of divine mystery, to cling

to the bible stories that offer release
to the captives, walk the barrios from

end to end with the tiny drop of bread
that makes silenced lands new and

bite my tongue while singing with a
wide smile, Aleluya, ¡gloria a Dios!

you will not believe me when I say
the buildings vomit when Cathedral

bells ring to spread news of a God
who does not give us light. it will

only take an hour of life with us in
the country where brown flesh turns

cold to understand heresy on these
forgotten streets has no time for

churchy preaching.

THE CARAVAN

the walk is charged with
the presence of the Highest,
the stranger from afar now in
flight, feeling a divine way with
precious lives bent and hidden
in those who build themselves
dreams. the darkest part of the
journey ahead is the border with
soldiers who wait with stones in
hand, these neighbors who can't
hear the prayers in our heads, see
their own callous crimes nor admit
children's shattering cries. the president's
men, the misfits, chiselers, high class
criminals and tickertape frauds will
never stop the coming of God's own
trodden down. O yes, Herodian thugs,
blessed are the poor!

THE NATIONALIST

we woke up this morning
inspecting from these cells
puncturing undocumented
flesh the country going out
of its way to mortally wound
us. we will inhale American
air full of hate, the procession
of White House lies that creep
by the cries of our separated
children, smells of this nation's
withering dreams and the aroma
of incense carried by the small
group of citizens with signs of
rebellious peace. the nationalist
politicians keeping us in prison,
their sinister disorder, long closed
eyes, blood-soaked hands and
stinging tongues never loved the
resurrection that brought us this
far. we woke up this morning to
pound some more on our neighbor's

door, to share new questions with
stammering tongues, demand from
a supposed Christian nation a tiny
fleck of love, and say some day
our truths will be hung in your
precious museums!

AMERICAN PIE

we sit on a foggy night
resurrecting the expired

by simply calling their
dear names: Olga,

María, Emilia, Miguel,
Jacob. we plan to talk

into the night until the
dawn finds us, slowly

sharing thoughts dipped
for generations in Latin

American sorrow, letting
them crawl the apartment

floor until they recall the
prayers given to each of

us by old village priests.
we walked hundreds of

miles, listen to Spanglish
shout from our U.S. born

kids, marvel about people
here afraid of our brown

skin and wonder what the
citizens think about the

future tangled up now in
so much shit! sometimes,

we sit in silence like a small
group of strangers in church

for the first time wondering
what God really has time to

save us or deserves tonight
a word of thanks.

PRAGMATISM

remember the night after you
got home from the toy factory

work, the dim lighted hallways
of the building panting from so

many years of foreign languages
dancing on its walls, the mailbox

on the first floor where you looked
for news from a faraway land yet

empty to make you weep and the
way you sat down on the old worn

out couch with centuries of fatigue
showing on your face. your children

who dreamt of coming out somewhere
have never forgotten that old tenement

space on West Farms Road, the living room
that never got enough light, and the unbearable

feeling of uncertainty that blew through
the cracks on the apartment door and the

fire escape window. do you remember the
Cathedral steps you liked to stand on though

you refused to attend Sunday mass, the many
times you explained that God disappears in

the sanctuary dark, and how you tried to convince
Holy Week penitents Angels go up in flames when

listening to the well-practiced homiletical lies
tossing the poor into fiery lakes. remember when

your youngest brown faced son said close your eyes
and when they open everything will change—we

know you still have them closed.

THE SALE

I learned the block was up
for sale to anybody with a

check book though no one
stepped forward to make a

bid. the news traveled fast on
Southern Boulevard making

eyes big, the piragua vendors
were chatting about it hoping

their favorite restaurants were
included in the price and thinking

about applying for a joint checking
account at the Dollar Savings Bank

accepting tiny sums of Puerto Rican
cash. two shoe shine boys got into a

philosophical discussion about what
it would mean to own the block and

where neighborhood improvement
needed to begin. a grandmother who

was coming out of the local A&P
with a bag of groceries in a two-wheel

push cart got the news too and she
told the little kid helping her for a

fifty-cent tip just find other things
to gratify your prayers for daily bread

for this block will please non-Spanish
speaking needs in this sale until the

world drifts toward its appointed
end—the little boy who knew the

Lord's prayer in sleep pondered
for the rest of the walk.

www.ingramcontent.com/pod-product-compliance
Lightning Source LLC
Chambersburg PA
CBHW070240230426
43664CB00014B/2365